PROJECT INC. REVISITED

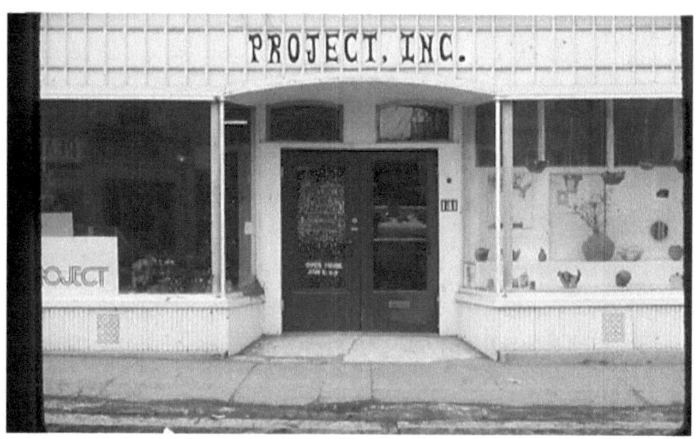

Printed in the United States of America.

First Printing, 2012
ISBN 978-0-9881895-1-5

Churner and Churner
205 10th Avenue
New York, NY 10011
www.churnerandchurner.com

PROJECT INC. REVISITED

edited and designed by Ian Wallace
text by Paul McMahon

published in conjunction with the exhibition
Project Inc. Revisited
at Churner and Churner
205 10th Avenue
New York, NY 10011
July 2 - 7, 2012

CHURNER and CHURNER

TIMELINE OF EVENTS

11/24/72	ROBERT (C) MORGAN
12/8/72	PAUL McMAHON
12/15/72	DAN GRAHAM
12/22/72	JACK GOLDSTEIN
12/29/72	JAY JAROSLAV
1/12/73	DOUGLAS HUEBLER
1/19/73	JAMES WELLING
1/19/73	VIDEOTAPES BY CAL ARTS STUDENTS
1/26/73	DONALD BURGY
2/18/73	TOM MARIONI
2/24/73	JOHN KNIGHT
3/3/73	AUDREY ADNEY
3/3/73	GREGORY AMENOFF
3/29/73	WOLFGANG STOERCHLE
4/7/73	MARTHA S. WILSON
5/12/73	LAWRENCE WEINER
5/19/73	DAVID ASKEVOLD
5/25/73	RICHARDS JARDEN
5/26/73	TIM ZUCK
8/18/73	MICHAEL ASHER
10/20/73	DEAN NIMMER
11/10/73	POSTCARDS, COLLECTED AND SENT BY ARTISTS (TRAVELED TO OBERLIN COLLEGE SOON AFTER)
11/17/73	BRUCE ANDREWS
12/1/73	MATT MULLICAN
1/16/74	FIVE BOSTON CONCEPTUAL ARTISTS AT THE BOSTON ICA
4/4/74	J.B. COBB
5/4/74	ATHENA TACHA
5/11/74	ALICE AYCOCK
5/24/74	SOL LEWITT
7/27/74	LAURIE ANDERSON
7/27/74	GERRY HOVIGIMYAN
9/9-15/74	INDIAN SUMMER; MCMAHON, MORGAN, MULLICAN, WELLING, SALLE
11/16/74	EMMANUEL KELLY
12/7/74	ALAN SONDHEIM
12/17/74	JAMES WELLING PLUS 'BOATYARD' INSTALLATION AT MASSART
FEBRUARY 1975	CHARLES SIMONDS
2/6/75	VIDEOTAPES AND A PERFORMANCE AT THE BCAE; MULLICAN 'ESSEX', HUDSON-TAVA, NIMMER-AMENOFF
2/16/75	MATT MULLICAN PERFORMANCE AT MASS ART
3/1/75	WILLOUGHBY SHARP
3/15/75	DAVID SALLE
4/1/75	ALAN SONDHEIM
APRIL/MAY 1975	PETER DOWNSBROUGH ERNST CARAMELLE
7/26/75	BARBARA HERO
7/26/75	ROBERT (C) MORGAN

CONTENTS

Introduction

Group shows
ordered chronologically

Solo shows
ordered alphabetically

Image credits

Acknowledgements

Introduction
Paul McMahon

It was at Project Inc., between 1972 and 1975, that Conceptualism passed the baton to the new post-Conceptual art in the form of one-day exhibitions and events by an impressive roster of Conceptual and Performance artists.

-Douglas Eklund, *The Pictures Generation 1974-1984*

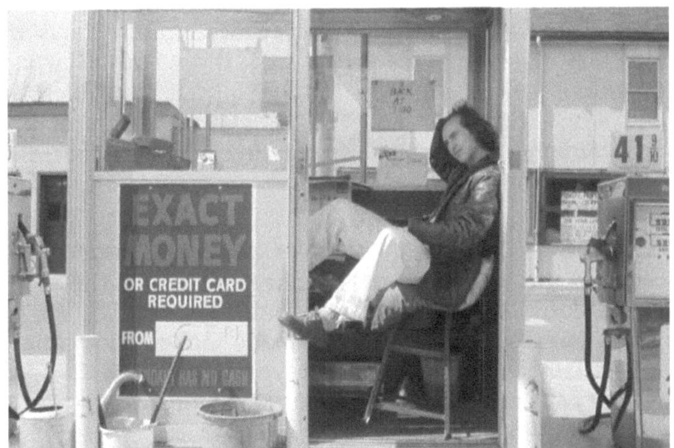

Paul McMahon at his job as a gas station attendant in 1972

Forty years ago, from December 1972 until July 1975, a series of over 30 art shows at a little storefront called Project Inc. introduced conceptual art to the Boston area and provided the first look at the new post-conceptual sensibility of my peers who would be dubbed the Pictures Generation. Douglas Eklund used that name for his retrospective of the early years of this group at the Metropolitan Museum in 2009: *The Pictures Generation, 1974-1984*. This series included the first Boston performance of Laurie Anderson, the first solo show of David Salle, and first Boston shows of Lawrence Weiner, Dan Graham, Michael Asher, and many others.

In 1972 I had just graduated from Pomona, where I studied with Mowry Baden, Helene Winer, James Turrell, and Hal Glicksman. In the course of my studies I also benefited from contact with John Baldessari, David Askevold and Barbara Reise. I was completely committed to post-studio/conceptual art; living and breathing it 24/7. I thought of art almost as a philosophical or religious cause, a way of breaking free of habitual thinking.

When I returned to Boston I found a provincial capital which conceptual art had not yet penetrated. Around the corner from me at 141 Huron Avenue, not far from Harvard Square, there was a little storefront space called Project Inc., a neighborhood art center that offered afterschool art classes for children. They also had a ceramics studio and darkroom that were open to the public on a walk-in basis. They offered a few types of classes, and I proposed giving some lectures there on conceptual art. The director, Trintje Janssen, liked the idea and I made a poster for the lecture series: 3 EVENINGS OF NON-STUDIO ART. It didn't fly, but I had made a good connection and soon had a better idea: art shows!

I proposed the following deal to Trintje. She would give me the keys when Project closed at 6 PM on a Friday or Saturday and when she came in the next day the place would look the same. That was it. No rent, no questions asked. Nobody thought about insurance then. The arrangement worked for her and thus ensued a series of around 30 shows in a funky little white space in a quiet, out-of-the-way neighborhood in Cambridge.

I'd go in at six with the artist and take down the fingerpaintings, or whatever was on the walls and neatly put it all away. Then we'd install the show. The doors would open at 8 and close at 10. We'd put the fingerpaintings back up and voila! The place looked the same the next morning when Trintje opened up. I never heard any complaints but there must have been at least one kid who wondered why his fingerpainting was upside down.

I was just barely able to afford to do the shows. I figured the whole cost of a show was in the range of $30. My fulltime gas station job paid $80 a week but my apartment was just $35 a month (the gas station owner was also my landlord). The use of Project Inc. was free and roundtrip trainfare from New York for the artist was only $20. In addition, Project Inc. had a bulk mailing permit (1.4 cents apiece) so the printing and mailing to the list of about 300 people came to under $10 a show. The artists stayed in the apartment I shared with my future wife Jody and we fed them. I never made a penny from the shows until the Center for Curatorial Studies at Bard College acquired the archives in 2010. But I did get hired in 1975 to be Assistant Director at Artists Space by my mentor and friend Helene Winer.

The one night format was, of course, natural for performance art, film, or video, but unusual for visual work. However, I had spent enough time in art galleries to know that upwards of 90% of the people who see a show see it at the opening. So I reasoned I could just have the opening and it would accomplish more or less the same end without all of the overhead.

I was interested in a lot of artists who lived in New York and had been making it my business to meet them. Most of them wanted to show in Boston. The only ones who already had were Sol Lewitt, who had done something at MIT, and Doug Huebler, who lived in the area.

Helene Winer's program of exhibitions at Pomona was my main inspiration for showing art at Project Inc. and Dan Graham was the most supportive and helpful to me of all of the artists of his generation. I may have done something interesting without their help but I might not have, too. Dan's assistance was invaluable. He gave me his mailing list and introduced me to his friends, many of whom showed in the series, like Sol Lewitt, Lawrence Weiner, and Michael Asher. These artists, so well known today, were unknown then outside of a small circle of gallerists, critics, curators and artists, mostly in New York and Europe. Virtually no one in Boston was aware of conceptual art at all and I was not able to get the attention of the local art reviewers. I am not very aggressive when it comes to beating the drum about my activities. Maybe someone else could have gotten more play in the press. Dan's mailing list, augmented by about thirty Boston addresses and a few from other artists, came to about 300 people. The majority were in New York, with a couple of dozen in LA and Europe. A number of people have said that this list was practically the entire worldwide audience for conceptual art at the time.

In the end I followed a different drummer and did not pursue a career either making or showing art. My last day at Artists Space was 7/7/77, thirty-five years before the last day of Project Inc. Revisited. I remained true to my inner promptings and undertook a course of psychological healing, which led seamlessly into a spiritual journey, resulting in my life today as a Renaissance person and part-time mailman living in Woodstock.

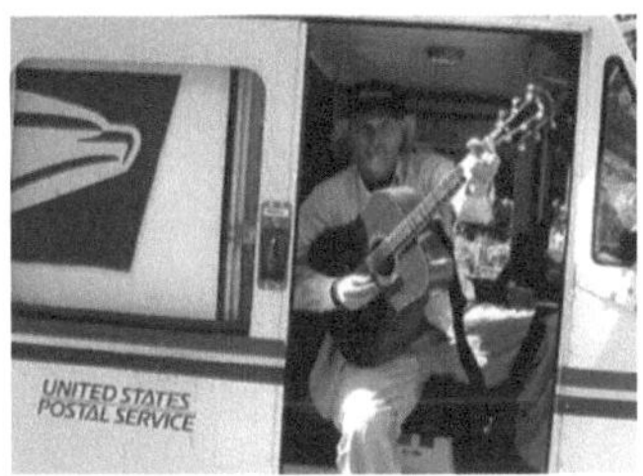

Postcards By Artists
November 10, 1973

re/ Show of Artists' Postcards
at PROJECT INC.
Cambridge, Ma.
02138

Dear

As you are probably aware, many contemporary artists collect and send unique, interesting postcards.

These cards reflect, to some degree, the sensibilities of their senders, so they have artistic interest. They are interesting in themselves and also as documents. Also, the fact that so many artists are now collecting them constitutes a minor phenomenon in itself.

Therefore I will be doing a show of selections from artists'postcard collections at Project Inc. this Fall. Tentatively scheduled for late September/ early October, the show will include selections from 15-25 collections.

If you collect postcards, you are invited to participate in the show. Please select the cards you would like to show and send them to me by September 10. The cards will be returned when the show is over. If there is private correspondence on the back of a card, it will be covered over by a piece of paper.

I hope to hear from you,
Paul McMahon

mailing address...... Paul McMahon
Cambridge School
Weston, Ma. 02193

SEPT 19, 1973

PLEASE USE THIS –

THE WORKERS HAVE NO ART FOR THE SAME REASON THE WORKERS HAVE NO WEALTH. ARTISTS IN AMERICA HAVE STOLEN THE ART OF THE WORKERS TO BUY THEIR OWN FREEDOM. CAPITALISTS IN AMERICA HAVE STOLEN THE WEALTH OF THE WORKERS TO PERPETUATE THEIR RULE. THANK YOU & BE WELL

@

ANDRE
BOX 540
NY NY
10003

SHOW OF ARTISTS' POSTCARDS
PAUL McMAHON
CAMBRIDGE SCHOOL
WESTON, MA. 02193

Carl Andre's contribution to the Postcards show, front and back, 1973

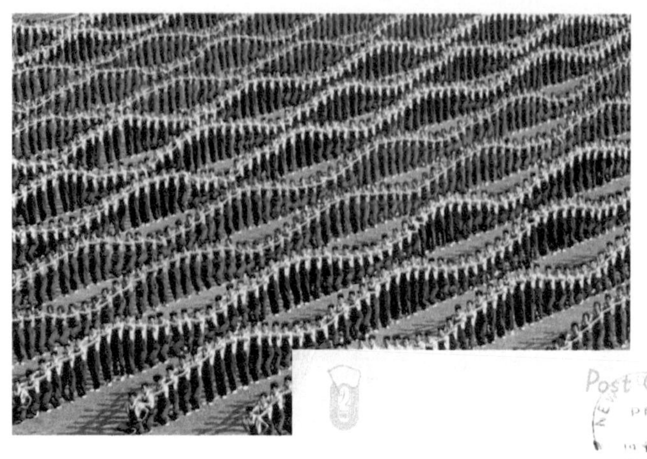

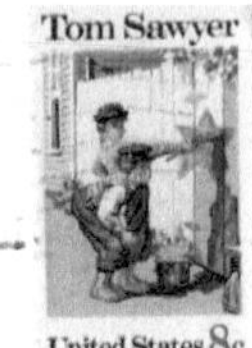

Postcard from Sol Lewitt, front and back with 'One Red Line From The Left', 1973

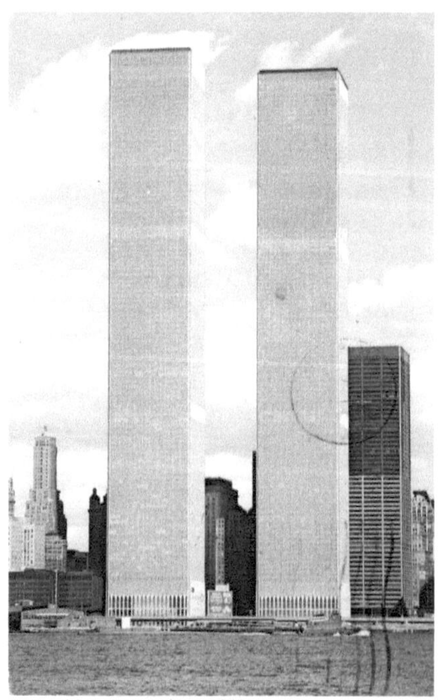

Postcard from Dan Graham, 1973

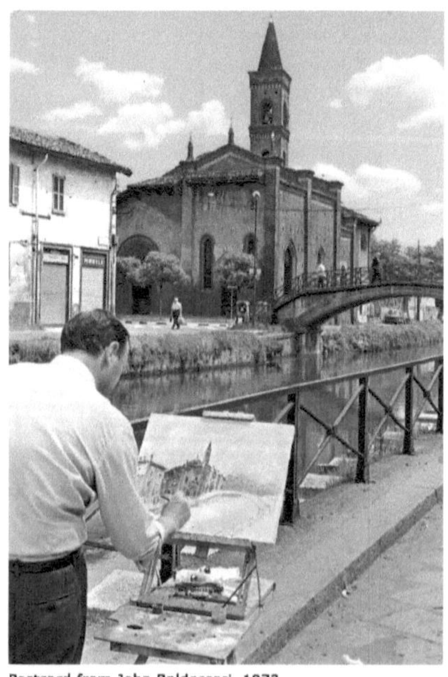

Postcard from John Baldessari, 1973

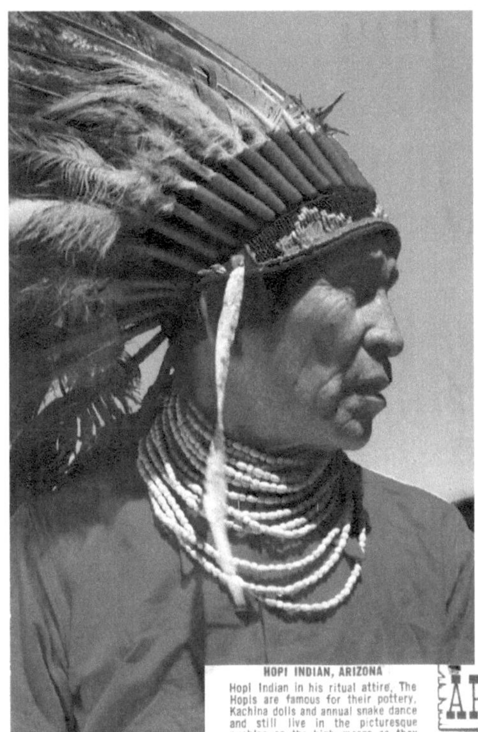

HOPI INDIAN, ARIZONA

Hopi Indian in his ritual attire. The Hopis are famous for their pottery, Kachina dolls and annual snake dance and still live in the picturesque pueblos on the high mesas as they have for centuries.

ARIZONA Mirro-Krome® CARDS

Address

Progress in Electronics

WILLOUGHBY SHARP
AS
THE MIGHTY MOGUL
ON THE EDGE OF THE CANYON

Summer of '73.

PROJECT INC
PAUL McMAHON
141 HURON AV.
CAMBRIDGE
MASS. 02138

MIRRO-KROME ® CARD BY H. S. CROCKER CO., INC., OKLAHOMA CITY, OKLA

PUBLISHED BY FRONSKE STUDIO, FLAGSTAFF, ARIZ. RMF-190

Postcard from Willoughby Sharp, front and back, 1973

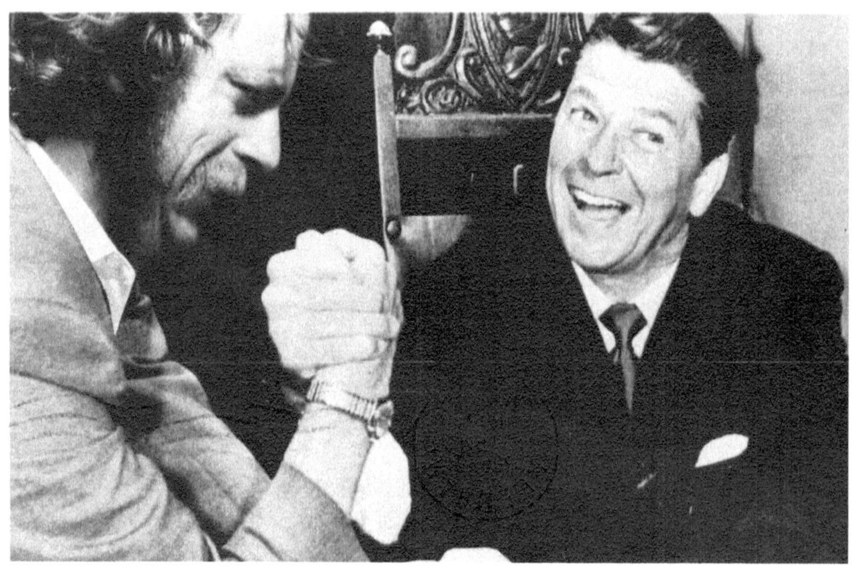

Postcard from Wolfgang Stoerchle, 1973

Five Boston Conceptual Artists
January 16, 1974 at the Institute of Contemporary Art, Boston

THE INSTITUTE OF CONTEMPORARY ART IN COOPERATION
WITH PROJECT, INC. PRESENTS
A ONE-NIGHT SHOW OF FIVE BOSTON CONCEPTUAL ARTISTS

BRUCE ANDREWS
DONALD BURGY
DOUGLAS HUEBLER
JAY JAROSLAV
ROBERT MORGAN

WEDNESDAY, JANUARY 16, 5-10 PM.
AT THE ICA, 955 BOYLSTON ST., BOSTON

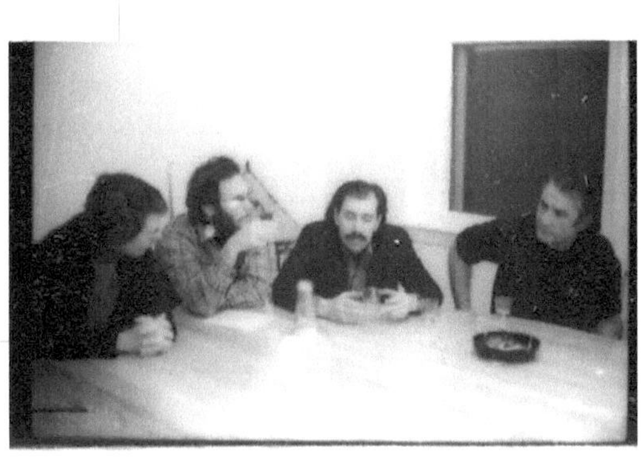

The statements that constituted Douglas Huebler's work in Five Boston Conceptual Artists were on sheets of fairly large paper (maybe 11 x 17 inches), unframed, pinned or taped at the top edge and not laying very flat on the wall. Not typeset, or even typed, the letters were printed freehand, in all caps, using a hot pink marker. They were conceptual art works that cared only for the presentation of the concept, and cared nothing about the packaging, framing, typesetting, etc. In other words, they were not market-driven in their intentionality, not seductively elegant, not something anyone would covet owning, apparently. This appealed to me as being true to the school of conceptualism as I understood it, which was noncommercial in nature, consisting, in its purest form, of the free flow of information. My own and my generation's intentions were quite different, but just as a person who is sexually active nonetheless condemns a priest or guru for sexual infractions, it sometimes seemed like conceptual art violated an implicit vow of celibacy by becoming overdesigned and perfect.

Above, from left to right: Robert C. Morgan, unidentified, Donald Burgy, and Douglas Huebler

Videotapes and Performance
February 6, 1974 at the Boston Center for Adult Education

Her father dies, sudden grief
The backyard flooded during a heavy rain
Looking at herself in the mirror
Her son's marriage
Brushing her teeth
Starting a garden
Her daughter's graduation
The broken glass in the basement door
Swimming
An itch in the lower part of her back
Her daughter's school in a foreign country
Spending half the year at the ocean
Looking at a photograph of herself as a child
Being scared to enter a dark room
Having a grandchild
Feeling older
Remembering schooldays
A glass of water
They have retired
Their son's independence
Touching herself
Cooking a "hearty meal"
Forgetting her age
Their house
Going for a trip around the world
Hair turning white
Her daughter's marriage
Working at her desk
Wondering where that person lives
Being visited by her daughter-in-law's parents
Noticing that the sky is a light shade of blue
The red car down the block
Catching her breath
Watching T.V.
Taking a nap in the hot sun
Her husband dies
Moving
Thinking about her eventual death

Partial view of the text of *Essex* by Matt Mullican

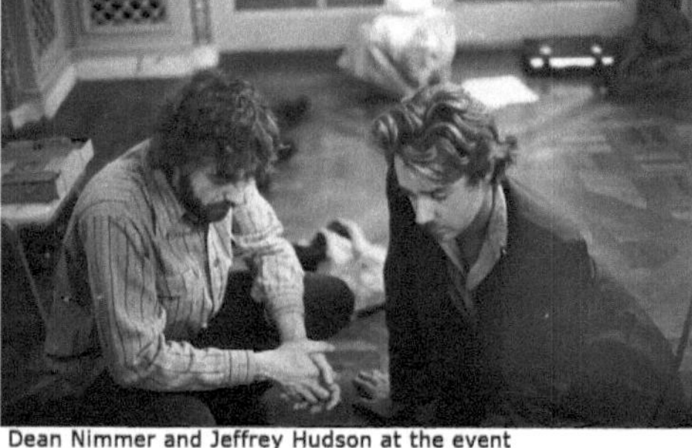
Dean Nimmer and Jeffrey Hudson at the event

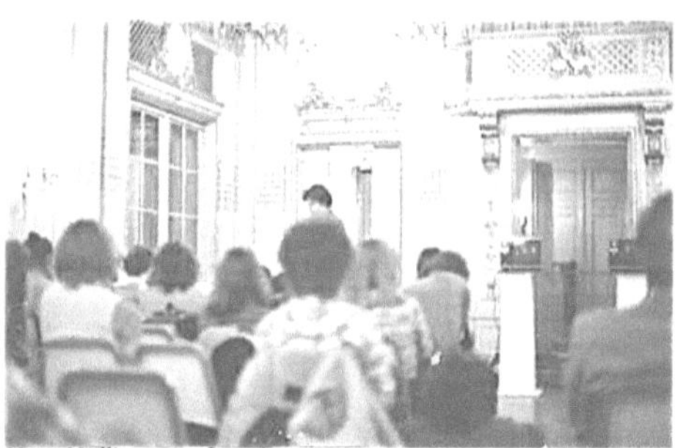
Matt Mullican performing

One of the places where I unsuccessfully tried to teach a course in conceptual art, the **Boston Center for Adult Education**, hosted an evening of performances. By far the best attended of any of the events I organized during these years, it featured video and performance by local artists Hudson and Tava, Dean Nimmer, and Greg Amenoff, respectively. It also included a powerful and emotional performance of *Essex* by Matt Mullican.

Indian Summer

Paul McMahon, Robert Morgan, Matt Mullican, David Salle, and James Welling

September 9 - 15, 1974

The work shown in "Indian Summer" represents a new sensibility -beyond Conceptual Art.
As students, four of the artists studied under Conceptual Artists and each has an a priori understanding of Conceptual Art to which he is reacting.
Although the work is strongly idea-oriented, the visual image is much more important than in Conceptual Art. The pieces also have emotional and mysterious qualities which most Conceptual Art lacks.
The works are more objects to be seen and experienced than vehicles for specific ideas.

Paul McMahon
Director of Art Shows
Project Inc.

This description is extremely generalized and I do not presume to be speaking for the other artists.

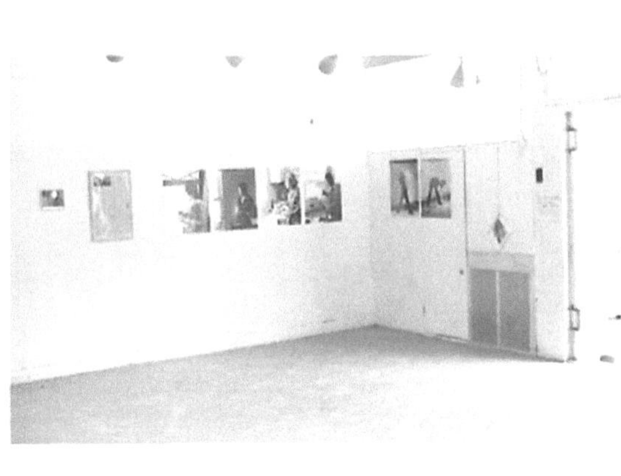

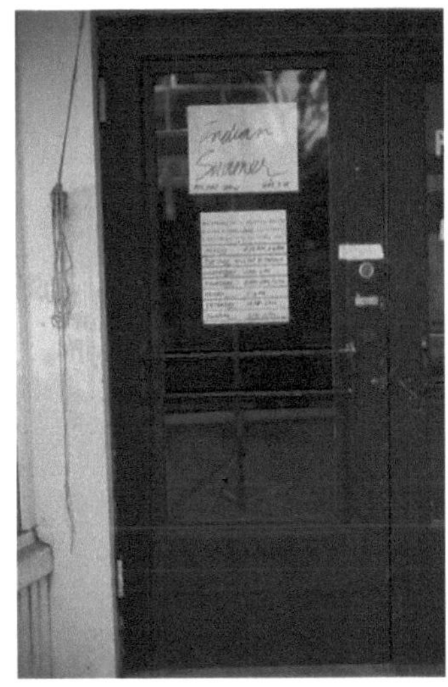

Above, installation, including David Salle's *Coffee Drinkers*, and exterior view of Indian Summer at Project Inc., 1974

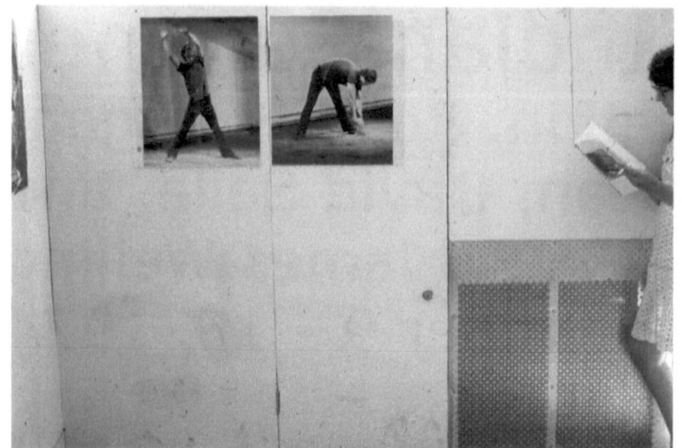

Installation view with a piece by Robert C. Morgan

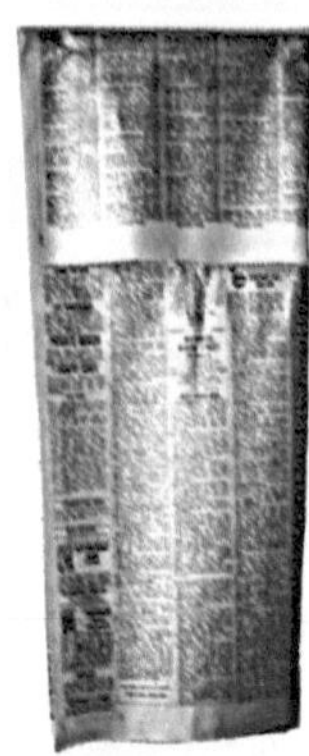

Matt Mullican, *Head and Body*

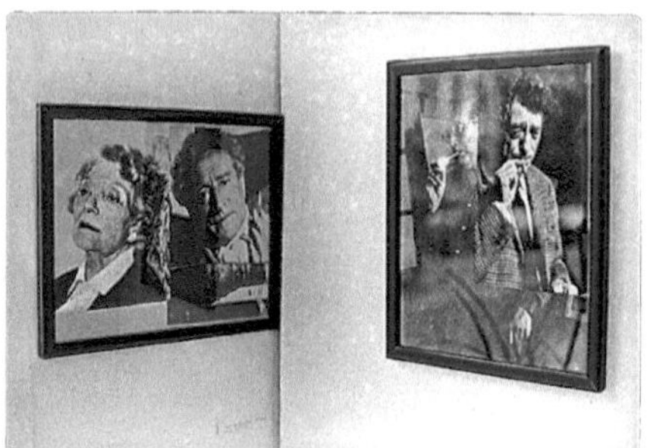

James Welling, *Jean Rhuys, Jean Cocteau* and *Mark Rothko, Alberto Giacametti*, installation view, 1974

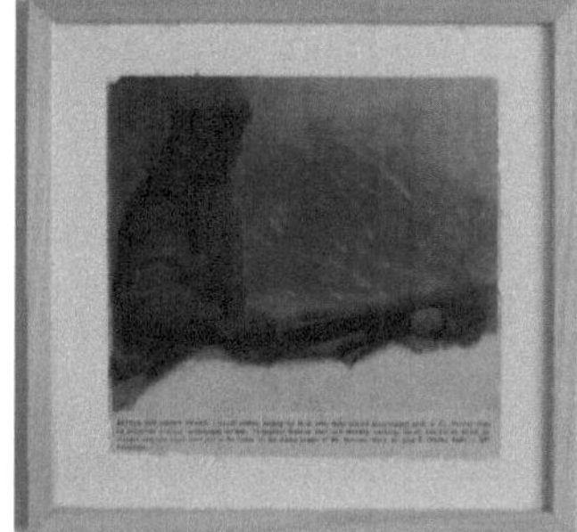

Paul McMahon, *Battle for Snowy Peaks (Israeli Soldier)*, pastel on newsprint, 1974

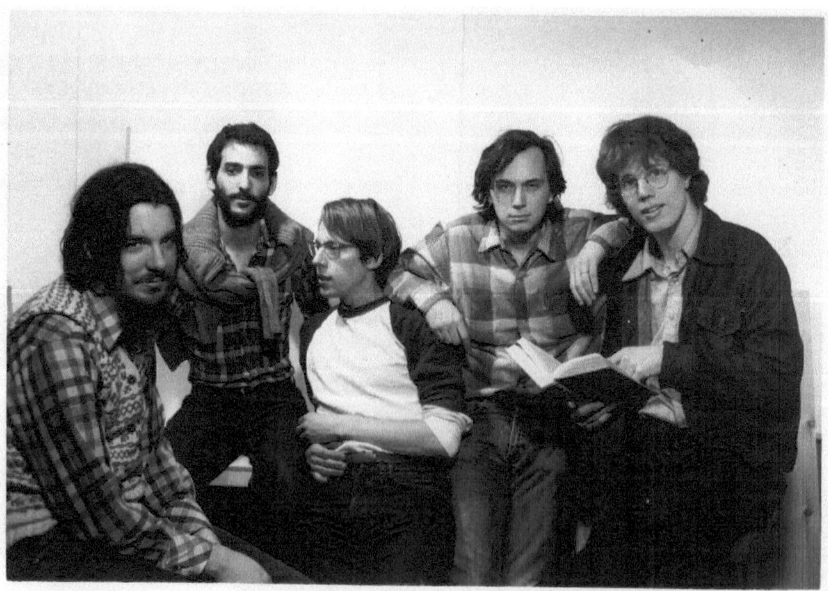

From left to right: Matt Mullican, David Salle, James Welling, Paul McMahon, and Robert C. Morgan

Carol Adney & Gregory Amenoff
March 3, 1973

Carol Adney (Audrey Adney), *Horsetail Whip*, 1973

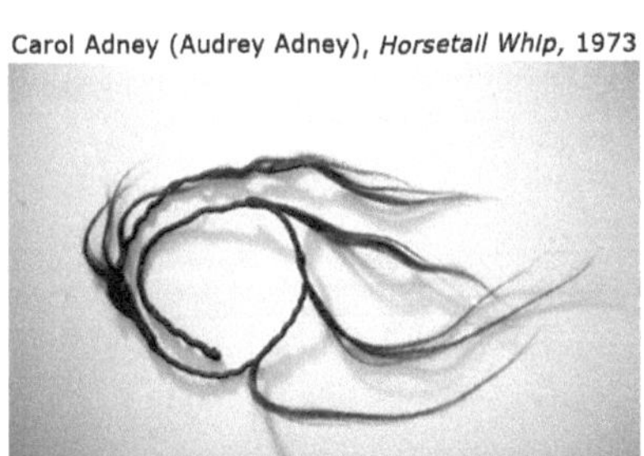

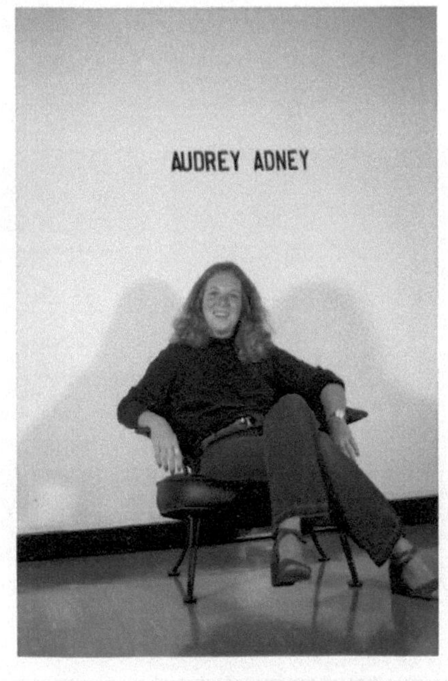

Carol Adney was my friend at college. I think she went to Scripps but gravitated toward the interesting things going on in the Pomona Art Gallery and Department. We exchanged ideas and one day we were sitting in this little shady out of the way spot on the Scripps campus. It was afternoon and that sort of timeless Pacific light was making the moment feel eternal. We hit on the idea of just not leaving. We realized that if we just sat there, sooner or later we would become famous for just sitting there. People would have to bring us food and we'd have to think about sleeping and going to the bathroom. It was a funny idea and we came very close to doing it but ... not quite. Carol got into the "life as art" thing and started calling herself Audrey Adney and her overall endeavor Artfact. She got a PO Box and a rubber stamp. Artfact Adney. Later she moved back to Indianapolis and worked in the art museum there. She arranged to have Helen Winer and Jack Goldstein (they were a couple) speak there and she gave me the first show of the newspapers with pastel on them in 1975. One was stolen off the wall. As the thief fled, museum guards fired guns at the escaping car. Terrified, the guy threw the picture into the bushes. He got away. One of the things Carol showed at Project Inc. was a beautiful black whip she had woven out of horsetail strands. She shared an evening with Greg Amenoff.

Above, Carol Adney as Audrey Adney, 1973

Gregory Amenoff was one of the few painters in Boston who was doing work I found interesting. He was also doing art-themed sketch comedy performances and videos in collaboration with Dean Nimmer, which I occasionally participated in and presented at the Boston Center for Adult Education. One of the few people in Boston who was interested in new ways of thinking about art, he came to a number of the shows at Project Inc. I went to his studio in the Roxbury ghetto in a place called the Egg Building. He was melting wax in coffee cans à la Jasper Johns. The floor near the painting wall was covered with encaustic an inch deep. He cut out a piece the size of a brownie, which I still have. His paintings looked like brown mud, usually with one or two details, like a thin band of gold leaf. We showed two of these paintings, large for those days, around six by six feet.

In 1974 he insisted I accompany him to see a little known rising talent, Bruce Springsteen, in a small hall in Boston. What a fabulous show! In my experience Bruce was second only to James Brown in terms of pure showmanship.

Laurie Anderson
July 27, 1974

Laurie Anderson came to my attention courtesy of Lucy Lippard, who put her into a show of women conceptual artists that I caught at the Boston ICA. Laurie's work was the most exciting work in the show, especially this wigged out portrait of the Queen of Punt, which may have only been in the catalog, which was on 3 x 5 cards and I recently sold for good money. Thanks, Lucy! She stood apart from all the others in that generational way I was so interested in and I decided to meet her. I probably got her number from Dan Graham. I went to her loft on 2nd St. between Avenues B and C. This was a terrifying neighborhood in those days and one of the pieces she showed at the ICA was a series of pictures of surprised men's faces. Laurie, like so many women in those days, was often lewdly propositioned on the sidewalk by leering men. Instead of ignoring it Laurie turned the tables on them, spinning around and shooting the camera right in their faces, sometimes catching them still talking, but always off balance, with a growing awareness that they were being made a fool of. This or something else may have attracted negative attention: a local gang soon broke into her place three times. The first time they stole everything valuable. The second time they trashed the place. The third time they knew she was home and they came for her but she hid and they didn't find her. Soon after that she moved.

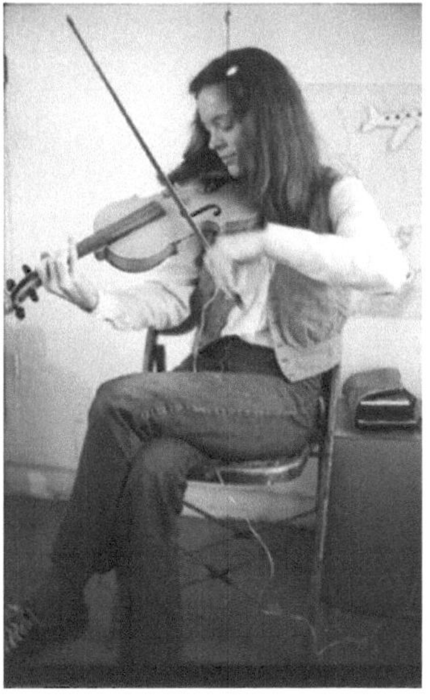

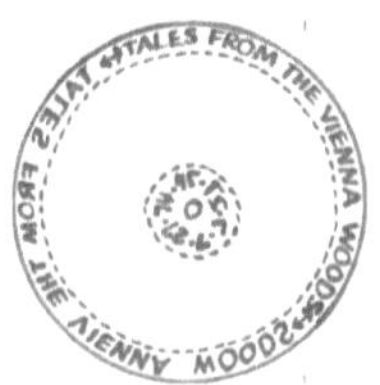

Laurie presented a wonderful performance with her violin of *Tales from the Vienna Woods*. It included a story of a train ride through the Vienna Woods, a sort of hypnotic weaving of a story that asks as many questions as it answers and doubles back on itself. She had already perfected her performance persona, which has remained remarkably consistent to this day. She said she thought of herself as the Doris Day of the art world. This was a historic event, being her first performance in the Boston area, but it was marred by something that only happened that once. She was mercilessly heckled throughout by Robert Horvitz, one of the most knowledgeable and sophisticated critics in Boston. To my knowledge he was the only Bostonian who could publish feature articles in *Artforum*, including a cover story on Chris Burden. God knows why he felt the need to do that to her at that time. It remains a mystery, unless he had a thing for her and this was his way of getting her attention.

Above, Laurie Anderson performing at Project Inc. 1974

Bruce Andrews
November 17, 1973

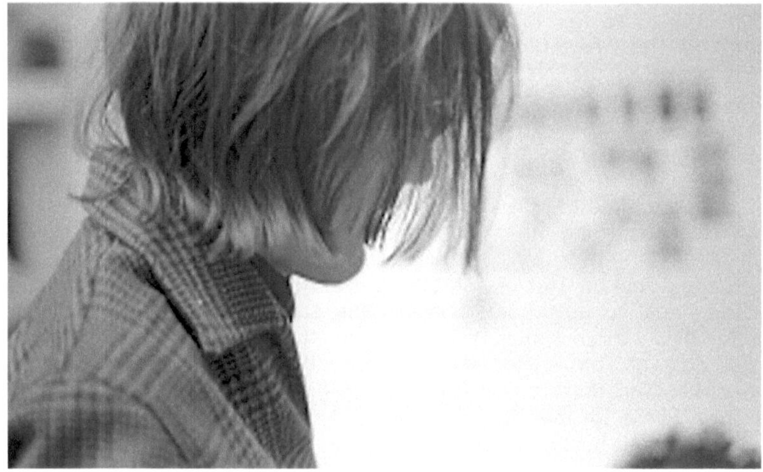
Bruce Andrews at Project Inc., 1973

Bruce Andrews contacted me after seeing something I put in a shop window in Harvard Square. Bruce immediately became an enthusiastic fan of the shows at Project Inc. His own interest was in something he may have called word-thing poetry, which is now called language poetry, after the magazine *L=A=N=G=U=A=G=E*, which Bruce edited. His show consisted of 3 x 5 cards with words hand printed on them placed all over on the floor and covered with a thin sheet of plastic so people could both walk on and read them.

Michael Asher
August 18, 1973

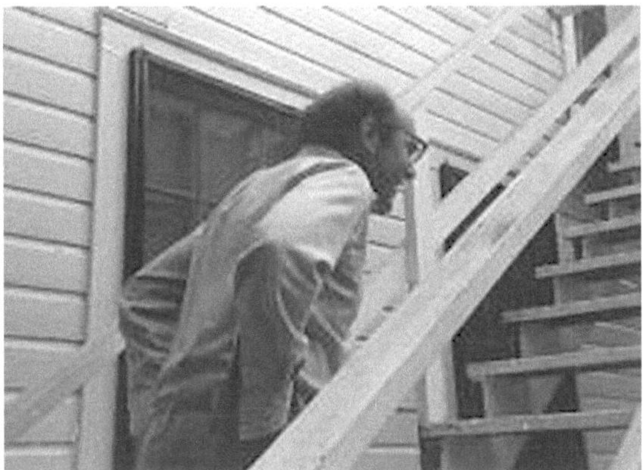
Michael Asher at the Cambridge School of Weston, Massachusetts, 1973

When I was a student at Pomona, **Michael Asher** installed one of the greatest art works I ever saw. During the installation I was assigned to take Michael to lunch at the dining hall. In the line he did something extraordinary. He was unable to choose between two vegetables being served. He couldn't decide if he wanted corn or carrots. But there was no question of not facing the problem head on. So he stood there and pondered every possible angle of the issue for several minutes as the dining hall line piled up behind him. It was amazing to watch. He finally made his decision and life went on as usual. But what it illustrated to me was his unflinching thoroughness and his categorical willingness to go to the limit on every tiny detail.

Michael was able to get a layover in Boston and he came to the Cambridge school to find an appropriate projection site for his film. He looked at a few places in the Trapelo House dorm and chose an unfinished room under construction, which had a good niche for a projector facing a blank white wall. Michael had made a film that was at one of the spectrum of what a film can be. The film was unexposed, but developed anyway. When projected, one saw the grains of the emulsion that had never received any exposure to light. And it could only be shown once because any time a film is run through a projector it inevitably gets scratched or marked.

There were only three or four people there for the showing of the film in 1973, including Jim Welling and myself. In 2005, after I'd been out of touch with the art world for a good long while, Matt Mullican notified me that Orchard in New York had decided to re-enact the Asher film screening. They went to great lengths to recreate the film as exactly as they could and projected it to a packed house. I was the only person to have been present for both screenings and they could hardly have been more different. At Orchard the overflow crowd was so respectful that it was as though it were a religious event. We were an awful lot more casual in 1973. I was surprised to come across a letter from him after he'd received the film back in which he seems to say he had projected the film again and also made a copy of it, which he felt was too light.

David Askevold
April 14, 1973

DAVID ASKEVOLD

April 14, 8pm

PROJECT INC.
141 HURON AVE.
CAMBRIDGE, MA.
02138
617-492-4438

NON PROFIT ORG.
U. S. POSTAGE
PAID
CAMBRIDGE, MASS.
PERMIT NO. 54240

David Askevold was a fascinating person. I met him in London in late 1971. I had been given an introduction to Barbara Reise, an American ex-pat and editor at *Studio International*. She took me under her wing and introduced me to David. He had been running the innovative "Projects" class at the Nova Scotia College of Art and Design, getting outside conceptual artists to send in assignments for his students. Barbara suggested that the three of us do a piece on college art education for *Studio*, which ended up being published as a conversation between David and me in the April 1972 issue.

I WAS READING A MAGAZINE WHILE ON MY WAY TO MEET A FRIEND IN DORANATO. I ASKED THE STEWARDESS FOR A CUP OF COFFEE. I REACHED IN MY BRIEFCASE TO FIND ANOTHER MAGAZINE, BUT DECIDED INSTEAD TO LOOK THROUGH SOME PICTURES AND LETTERS OF SOME PAST AND CONTINUING ACQUAINTANCES. I STARTED READING A LETTER FROM BILL DOWNING WHO SAYS HE IS IN SORTENDO DOING SOMETHING OR OTHER. I SIPPED MY COFFEE AND LOOKED OUT OF THE WINDOW.

A. I OPENED MY EYES TO A LIGHT GREEN WALL AND CEILING. FOR A WHILE I HAD A HARD TIME FOCUSING BUT B. I SAW THE BED I WAS LYING ON, C. A SMALL DRESSER, D. A LIGHT CENTERED ON THE CEILING, AND E. A SOUND WAS COMING FROM THE SEMI-OPEN WINDOW. I GOT OUT OF BED AND F. TRIED TO OPEN IT MORE BUT IT WAS STUCK. G. I COULD SEE THAT THE ROOM WAS ABOVE THE FIFTH FLOOR WHICH FACED THE BACK OF ANOTHER BUILDING. I COULD ONLY ASSUME THAT I WAS IN THE VICINITY OF DORANATO.

I RETRACED MY STEPS: 1. WALKING THROUGH THE CORRIDOR TO THE PLANE, 2. READING THE MAGAZINE, 3. ORDERING THE COFFEE, 4. REACHING IN MY BRIEFCASE, 5. SIPPING THE COFFEE AND 6. LOOKING OUT THE WINDOW. . . . a. COULD I HAVE LEFT THE PLANE AND b. SOMEHOW COME HERE FOR SOME REASON OR OTHER.

A. B. C. D. E. F. G.

b. a. 6. 5. 4. 3. 2. 1.

DORANATO–INITIATED–HALIFAX, FEBRUARY 1971–COMPLETED SAN FRANCISCO, FEBRUARY 1973

David was the first artist I had a chance to really hang out with. The wheels were always turning in David's head, and he thought differently, like a cat in a world of dogs. He had a kind of empty space in him that I attributed to a childhood in Montana. If I remember correctly he said at one time he became the executioner of unwanted pets in his small town.

He was no stranger to trouble. He had a studio fire in Nova Scotia around this time and was also fired from his teaching position. He later taught at CalArts and was a big influence on Mike Kelley, Tony Oursler, and others.

He was not able to come for his show. He mailed several pieces, simple photocopies of the 'rattlesnake herding' piece, a 'shoot/don't shoot' matrix, and some others.

Alice Aycock
May 4, 1974

ALICE AYCOCK
8 pm, May 4, 1974
Project Inc.
141 Huron Ave.
Cambridge, Ma.
891-5885

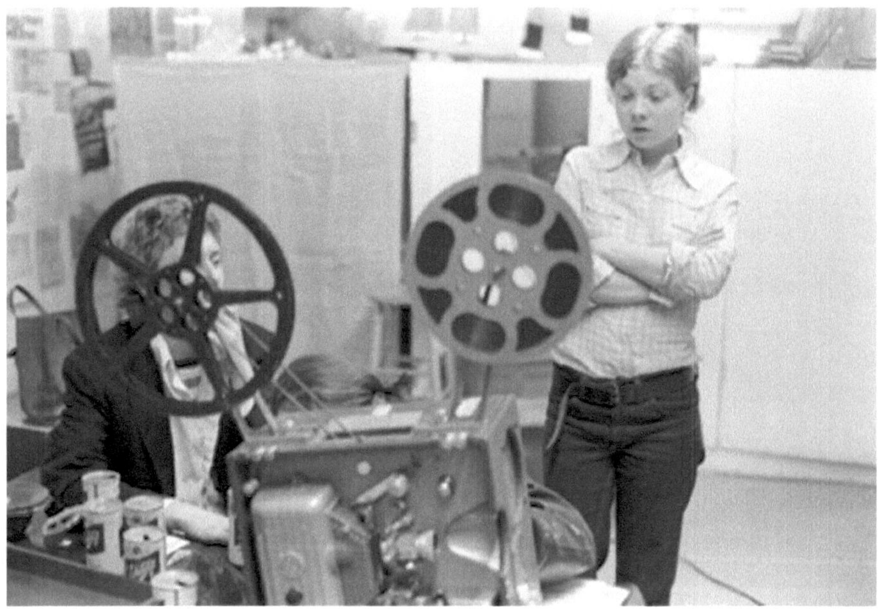

Alice Aycock was another artist whose work I saw in Lucy Lippard's *c. 7,500* show at the ICA. I don't remember exactly how the contact was made but it was certainly my intention to approach her about doing a show and I did. Given the "one night" nature of the gig, she decided she would focus on portable pieces of short duration. There was a palindromic 16mm film called *Midpoint* and a two-tape-recorder spoken word piece. Some of it was about Vlad the Impaler, the terrifying real life superfreak Romanian prince who was the inspiration for the fictional character Dracula. It was serious nightmare material.

Donald Burgy
January 26, 1973

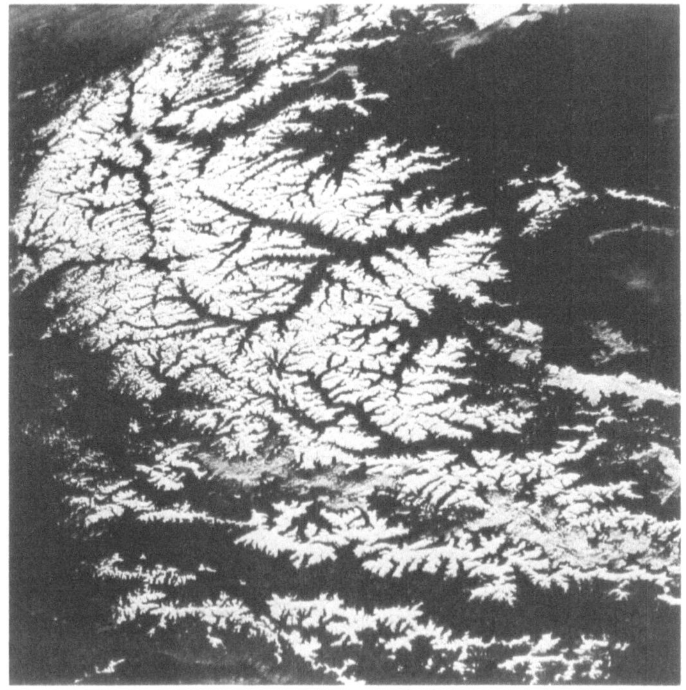

ALL FORMS OF ENERGY ARE IMPERMANENT.

For more than forty years, **Donald Burgy** has always incorporated science into his artwork. He is one of the founders of artscience.org, a site that explores this relationship. His show in 1973 was called *The Observer is the Observed*. He showed a work on large sheets of glossy paper that one leafed through, like a book. Each had a different photograph of part or all of the earth taken from outer space and a somewhat scientific statement about energy, like, "No two transformations of energy are exactly the same." The piece's title references a classic conundrum of the mind and body in quantum physics, as well as philosophy. I was surprised recently to learn that at around the same time, the quantum physicist David Bohm and the Indian philosopher Krishnamurti videotaped several conversations using "The Observer is the Observed" as their title. I first met Burgy through his good friend and associate Douglas Huebler when they were both teaching at Bradford College.

Above, Donald Burgy, *The Observer is the Observed*, 1973

Ernst Caramelle & Juan Navarro Baldeweg

June 27, 1975

Original description (translated from German):

1. The monitor shows an image of a hand with a hammer, hammering... silent (videotape recorded)
2. During the performance I am kneeling under the white cloth with covers the table. Through a hole I can see the Video image on a mirror attached on the opposite wall .... and try, hammering, to synchronize the silent (recorded) image with the (live) sound. (10 Min.)

- Ernst Caramelle

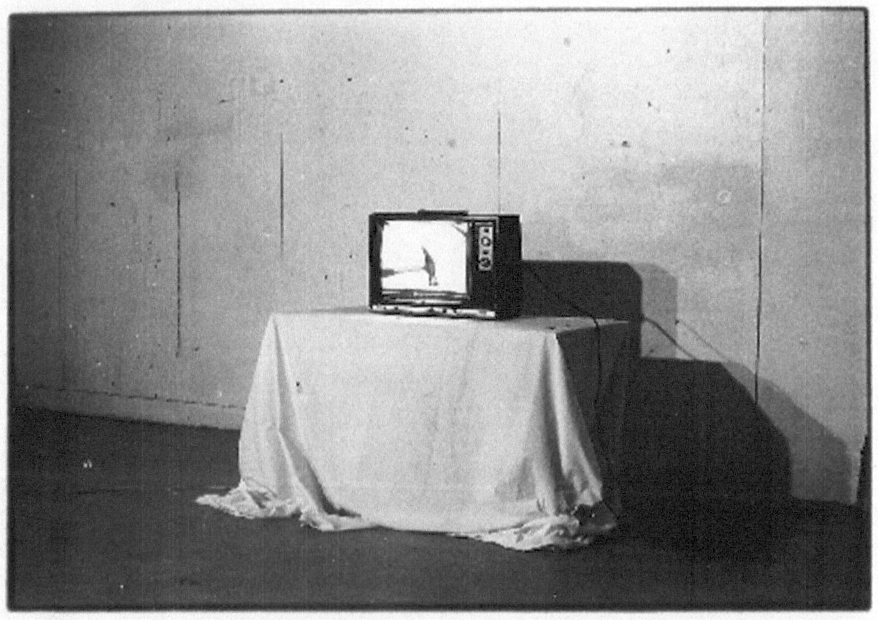

Ernst Caramelle was the only artist in the group who made a poster. He was also the only fellow at the Center for Advanced Visual Studies at MIT who took an active interest in the Project Inc. shows. He shared his show with Juan Navarro Baldeweg, a fellow fellow at the CAVS.

Above, Ernst Caramelle, *The Hammer Piece*, photo documentation of a performance at Project Inc., 1975

J.B. Cobb
April 6, 1974

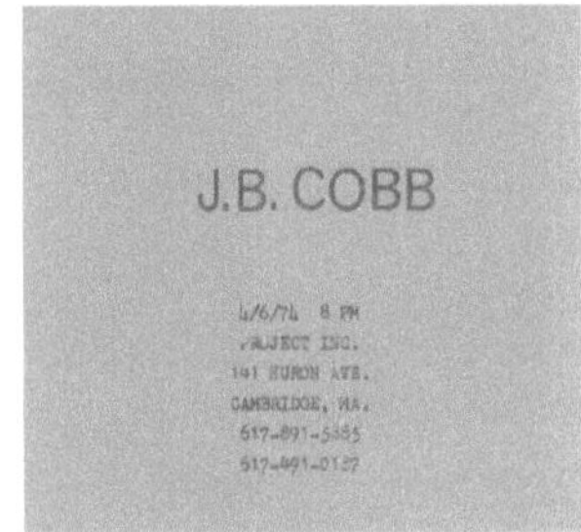

Peter Downsbrough
April/May 1975

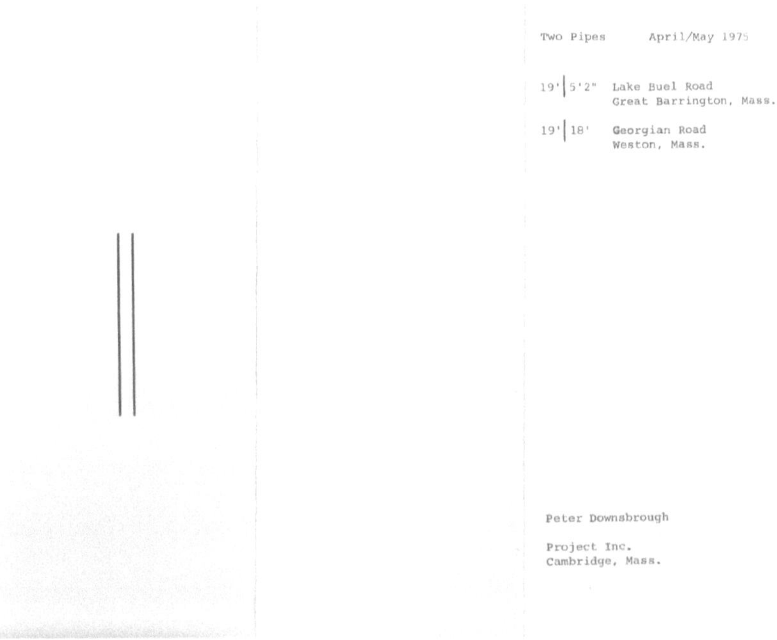

Peter Downsbrough printed his own announcement, an elegant minimal representation of two vertical lines on folded card stock. He installed two standing metal pipes on an untraveled part of the main lawn below Trapelo House at the Cambridge School in Weston. The standing pipes read as two parallel lines of uneven length in a landscape. I saw the work as a device for turning "reality" into "art." As I recall, the piece was still standing when we moved out a few months later in 1975.

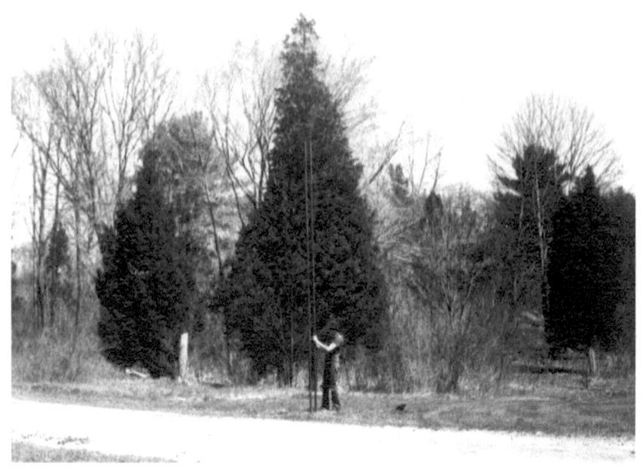

Peter Downsbrough installing his piece at the Cambridge School in Weston

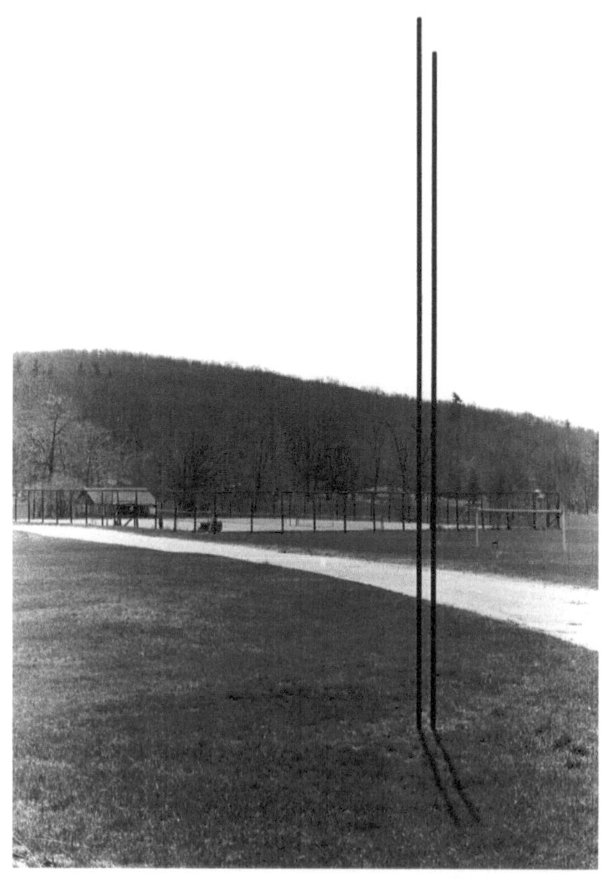

The view towards the athletic field

Jack Goldstein
December 22, 1972

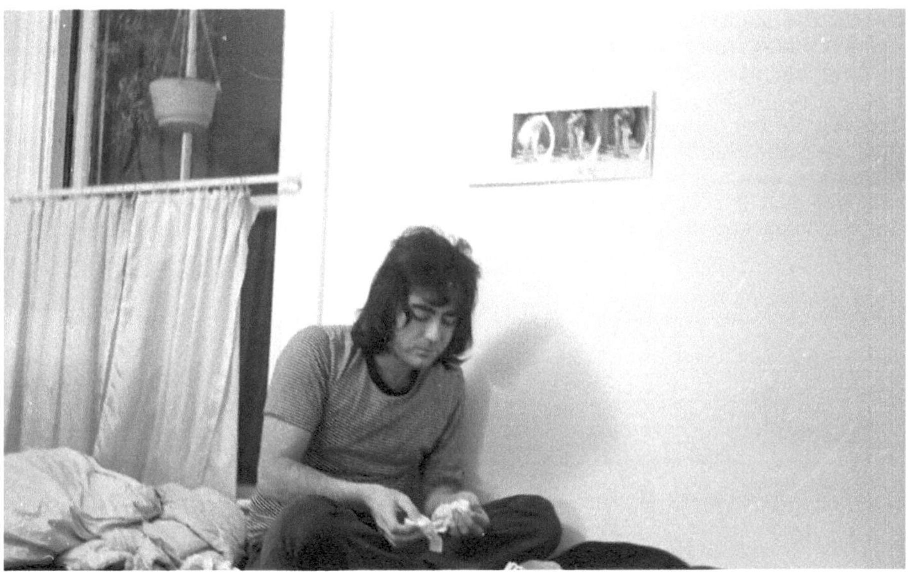

Jack Goldstein was probably the only LA artist who made the transition from the craft-oriented, ultra-clean LA sculpture/painting of the time to the conceptually grounded "Pictures" aesthetic that he helped co-create as a teaching assistant at CalArts. Jack always spent every nickel he had to produce his very expensive art works and his single-minded commitment to his work could be amusing. Whenever he had a new idea he would buttonhole you and tell it to you. This was inevitably followed by him looking you in the eye and asking, "Incredible, huh? Isn't it? Isn't it fantastic? It's the best, right? Can you believe it? Don't you agree? Right? It's my best work ever!" This happened with every artwork he ever did, both when it was a new concept, and after it was finished. He had made several black and white films by the time he showed at Project Inc., in December of 1972, but had yet to make the color films he is known for. He was also doing performances but they were not yet in the spectacular and colorful style of the later works for which he hired athletes and contortionists to perform under theatrical conditions with colored lights, etc.

At Project Inc. he showed some black and white 16mm films, including one of a dark card table with a full glass of milk on it. A fist pounds the table and some of the milk spills, making a white shape on the black tabletop. After awhile another blow spills more. This continues at a slow, deliberate pace several more times until the glass capsizes, leaving an abstract design of white on black. He also showed an installation, which was a kind of performing sculpture. The sculpture was made of two stepladders and two buckets, one with a small hole in the bottom. The ladders were set up so that their platforms were above one another. The higher bucket, with the hole in it, was full of water, which ran into the other bucket. One bucket slowly filled up as the other emptied, and this took place above the eye level of the audience. The stepladder piece was, I think, surprisingly unattractive to Jack. Coming from LA, where the aesthetic was so clean and everything was new, Jack had assumed, I think – although he did not say so – that the stepladders and pails would be brand new and the room would be the neutral, crisp white cube that one took for granted. Not so. We used the two funky old stepladders I was able to borrow and the room was nowhere near art world standards. A big fluorescent fixture was just a couple of feet overhead and only the perforated bucket was new, bought for the occasion.

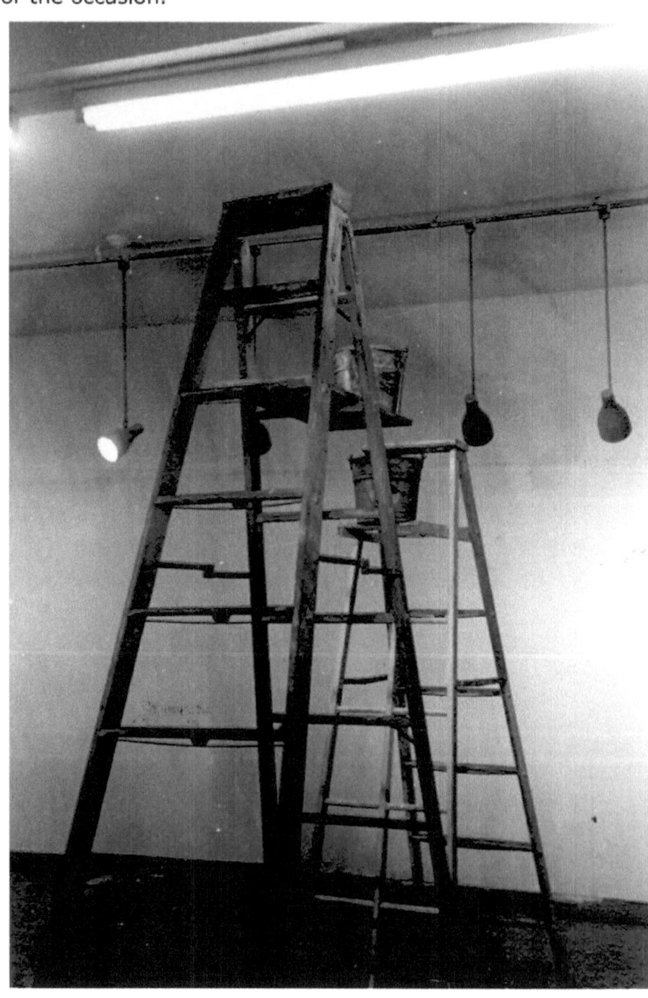

Dan Graham
December 15, 1972

FOR AUDIENCE'S REFERENCE:

intent (ME intent(us) an aim, purpose, literally, a stretching out) noun 1a. the state of mind or mental attitude with which an act is done b. an end or object proposed 2. Law, the state of a person's mind which directs his actions toward a specific object 3. meaning and signifigance

intent adj. 1. resolute, concentrated 2. having the attention sharply focused or fixed on something 3. set . syn.- CONCENTRATED, INTENSE, EARNEST

intention noun 1. the act or an instance of determining mentally upon some activity or result 2. an intended object 3. intentions, a). one's attitude toward the effect of one's actions or conduct 5. Logic, a general concept, especially, one obtained by abstraction from the ideas or images of sensible objects (first intentions), or one obtained by reflection and abstraction from first intentions (second intentions) - syn. - a goal

intentional, intentionality adj., noun Metaphysics 1a. pertaining to an appearance, phenomenon, or representation in the mind; phenomenal; representational b. pertaining to the capacity of the mind to refer to objects of all sorts, (intentionality) the characteristic of being conscious of intending an object

intentional object noun something whether actually existing or not that the mind thinks about: a referent of consciousness

Dan
Graham
performance
Dec.15

This is the third in a series of contemporary art shows, events and performances organized by Paul McMahon in co-operation with PROJECT INC. 141 Huron Ave* Shows will take place there every Friday night at 8pm throughout the foreseeable future. Important New York artists will show as well as Boston artists. $1 donation asked not demanded.

SCHEDULE INFO: Paul McMahon...492-4438
PROJECT INC....491-0187

*In Cambridge near Harvard Sq. On bus and trolley lines: Get off at the corner of CONCORD AVE and HURON AVE.

Dan Graham did a performance that dealt, among other things, with the nature of performance art. This piece appears in *Interfunctionen* magazine as it was performed at the Lisson Gallery in London. He also showed a 16mm film called *Sunrise to Sunset*.

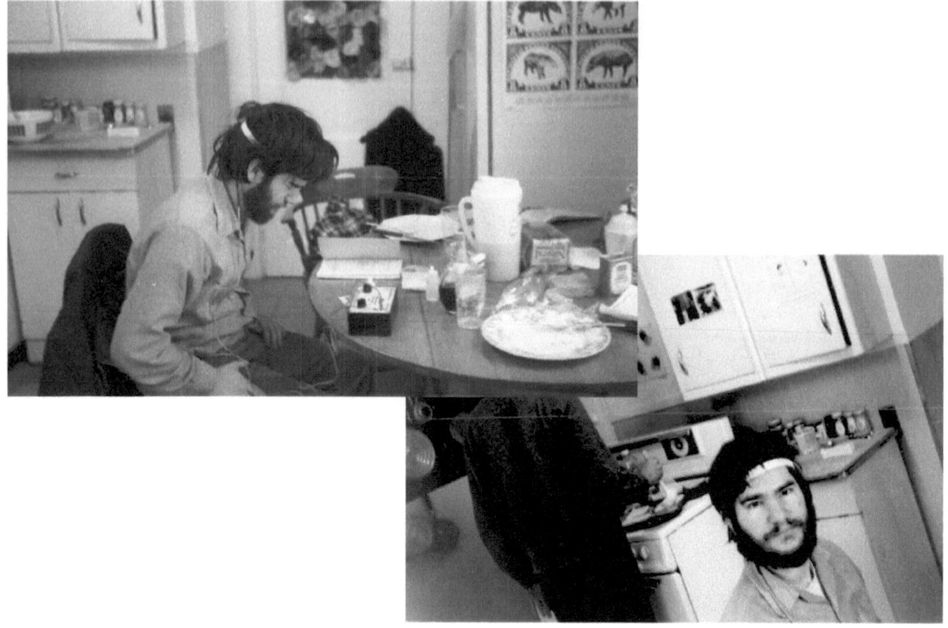

Dan was hyper-vigilant when it came to detecting, researching, and forecasting changes and developments in the culture. He was relentlessly theorizing on the ramifications of this and that. A subject he was fascinated by was the pseudo-science at the roots of Scientology and EST. In Scientology the goal was to be declared 'clear'. They had devices that they tested on people and that, as I understand it, mostly just measured galvanic skin response, the same thing measured in lie detector tests. This sort of device could be obtained from an outfit in Framingham, Massachusetts, which I think turned out to be called Silva Mind Control. Dan made it a condition of his showing at Project Inc. that I drive him there, which I, of course, agreed to. The time for that drive coincided with a vicious blizzard with large flakes of blowing snow. It was dark early (December) and the driving conditions were horrendous. There was no one but us on the road. The thirty mile trip was one of the most thrilling and dangerous of my life. Only crazy people would be out that night and we certainly fit that description. I was shocked to find Silva Mind Control open, but they were. Dan procured one of the galvanic skin response meters and we took it home to try it out. Jim welling was around then and can be seen in photos taken in the kitchen when Dan was trying way too hard to make alpha waves, which are best made by meditating or otherwise being so relaxed you are making no effect at all. Dan had a sort of anxiety driven intensity which caused me to go into my Mr. Relaxed persona, where none of the different things which were panicking Dan (at the rate of approximately one per minute) could disturb me, and I was able to sooth his fears and get on with the practical things that needed to be done. When I put on the GSR machine I made alpha waves right away, to the consternation of Dan, who hadn't made any. It was a very curious thing to base a pseudo-religion like Scientology on, but one could imagine how it might be an effective tool in a pseudo-religious setting where mind-control was the real goal.

GH Hovagimyan
July 27, 1974

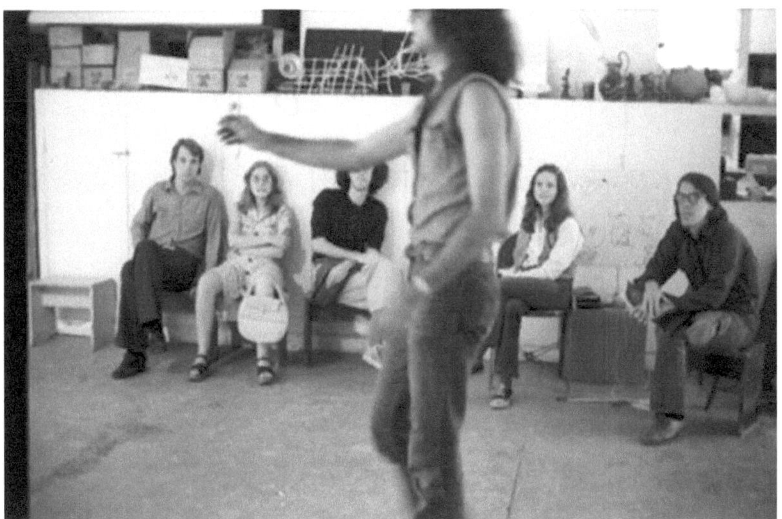

GH Hovagimyan performing at Project Inc., 1974.
In the background, from left to right: Greg Amenoff, unidentified, Robert Horvitz, Laurie Anderson, and Bruce Andrews.

GH Hovagimyan drove up with Laurie Anderson and did a performance before hers on the same evening. He went first, and the performance was a sort of sporting event that, if I remember correctly, consisted of him tossing darts at mousetraps, attempting to snap them shut. I also remember it being a sort of aggressive presentation with a sense of urgency and a "rant" component.

Douglas Huebler
January 12, 1973

DOUGLAS HUEBLER

AT PROJECT INC.
141 HURON AVE.
CAMBRIDGE near Harvard Sq.

FRIDAY JAN. 12 AT 8 PM
ONE EVENING ONLY
492-4438 491-0187

Douglas Huebler was the only Boston artist to be included in Seth Siegelaub's decisive catalogue *Six Conceptual Artists*. He showed a very early version of his piece that facetiously intends to document every person alive, a piece that he continued to work on for the rest of his life. He was not able to be present, but I was pleased that both here and in *Five Boston Conceptual Artists* at the ICA, the other show in this series that Doug was in, that he did not try to "clean up" the visual aspects of the work.

Richards Jarden with Tim Zuck

May 25, 1973

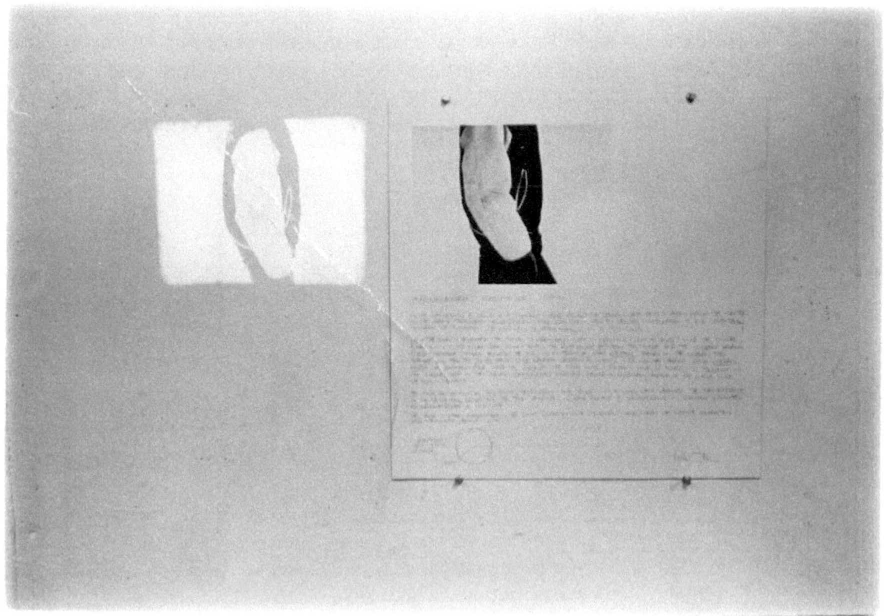

Richards Jarden, a dry wit, showed two versions of the same image side by side. He projected a film loop of a figure seen from the side from waist to shoulder wearing a letter jacket of the common variety, with a dark body and white sleeves. The camera pans along with the motion of the body so that the body is always walking but the frame composition stays the same, with the body filling the screen. Next to this was a photograph printed the same size as the projection on the wall of the same body framed the same way wearing the same jacket. So one image is walking and the other is a still photo of the walker. Jarden and his girlfriend Martha Wilson were both students at Nova Scotia College of Art and Design. So was Tim Zuck, who showed with Richards.

Jay Jaroslov
December 29, 1972

Jay Jaroslov is the son of an eastern European Jewish concert musician, but due to poverty he grew up in the ghetto in Bedford Stuyvesant, a rough section of Brooklyn. His work encompassed this divide in its combination of cultural sophistication and criminality. A teacher at the Museum School, he came to my apartment and gave me an extensive verbal account of his amazingly illegal oeuvre. His major work-in-progress was called *Extended Credentials*. He had acquired over thirty (fraudulent) identities, complete with birth certificates, drivers' licenses, passports, and more. He did this by an ingenious plan. In those days birth and death records were not correlated. Jay walked through the graveyards of Boston noting the names of boys who had died in infancy who would have been around his own age if they had survived. He then contacted area hospitals with letters claiming to be this person and requesting a duplicate birth certificate because his was lost. The hospitals were not as careful then, and he was issued over thirty of them, which he then used to obtain other forms of identification. He did astrological charts of them and invented personalities, professions, etc., for these fictitious people.

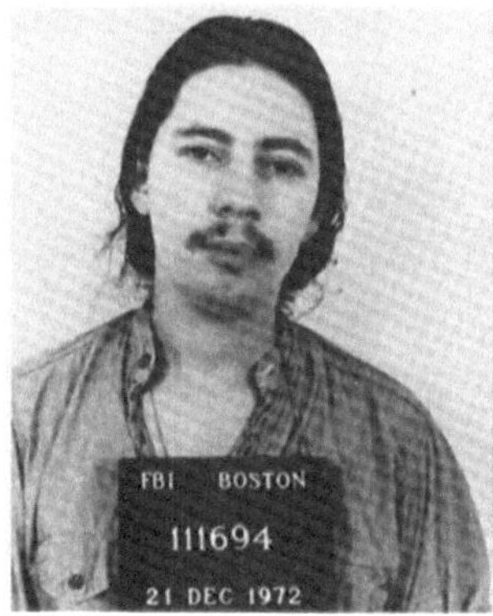

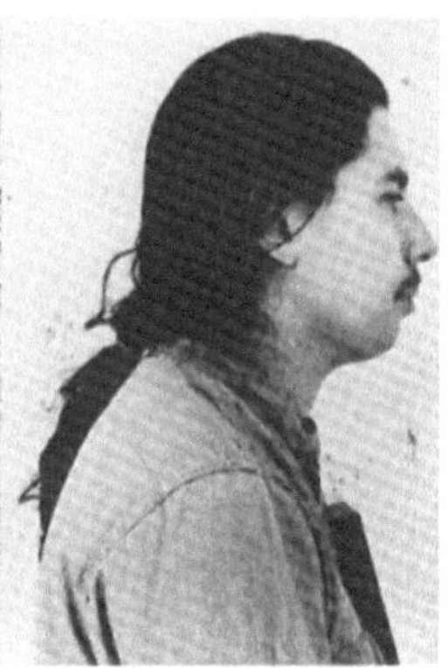

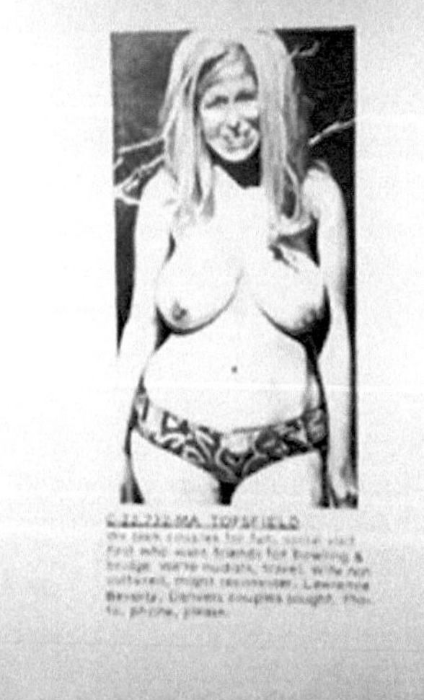

His proposal for his show was to **present work by** one of these people, Capotosto, whose chart indicated a likelihood of his becoming an artist. Capotosto was not the nicest person and his work consisted of large drawings of personal ads in "swinger" magazines. This was an early example of an artist using an opaque projector to make something small quite large. The swinger subculture of sexual adventurers, typically married to other swingers, advertised their desires explicitly with nude photographs of themselves. To take such information from a very private venue, blow it up, and show it in public was a definite invasion of privacy, although the chance of anyone making a personal connection with any of the swingers was very remote. They seemed to be from rural places in distant states. With less than a week to go before they show, the FBI arrested Jay, believing he was furnishing false identities to a ring of interstate car thieves, which was not true. We went ahead and showed the Capotosto work and Jay's arrest documentation from the FBI. Soon after this, he did a show of the arrest records and *Extended Credentials* at the Museum School, where he continued to teach. News of his arrest appeared in the same "Rumbles" section of *Avalanche* as the Project Inc. mention.

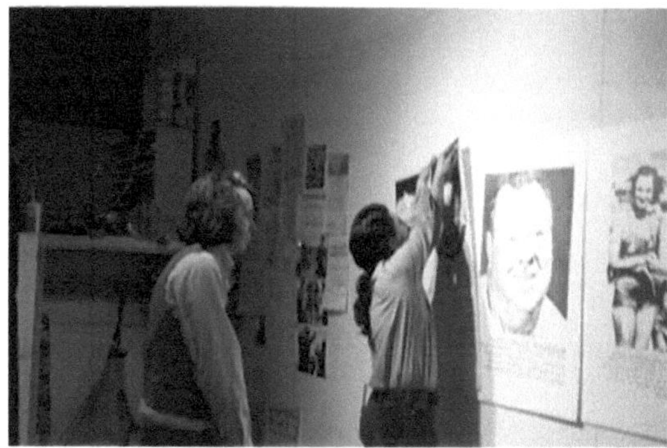

Jay Jaroslov installing *Extended Credentials*

Installation view

Emanuel Kelly
November 16, 1974

EMANUEL KELLY
Metaphors: Photos/Color
NOV. 16 AT 8 P.M.

PROJECT INC. 141 HURON AVE. CAMBRIDGE

John Knight
February 24, 1973

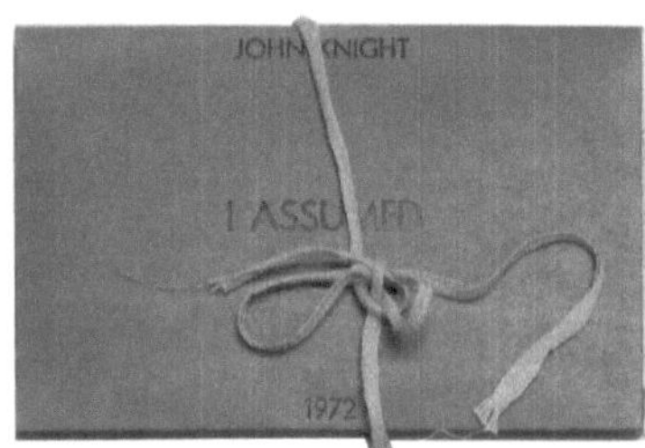
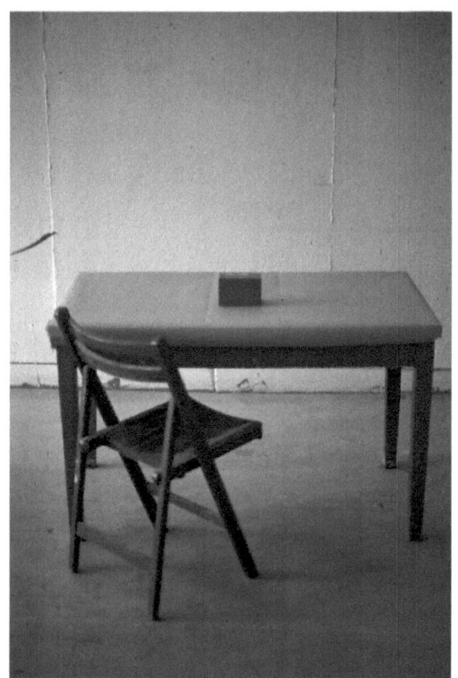

John Knight did a piece called *I ASSUMED... a work in situ*. While in New York he imagined what the Project Inc. space looked like and typed each assumption on a 3 x 5 card. For example, "The white paint on the radiator is beginning to peel." These cards were presented in a file box, on a table in the middle of the Project. Inc. space, creating a tension between the real and assumed spaces.

Sol Lewitt
May 24, 1974

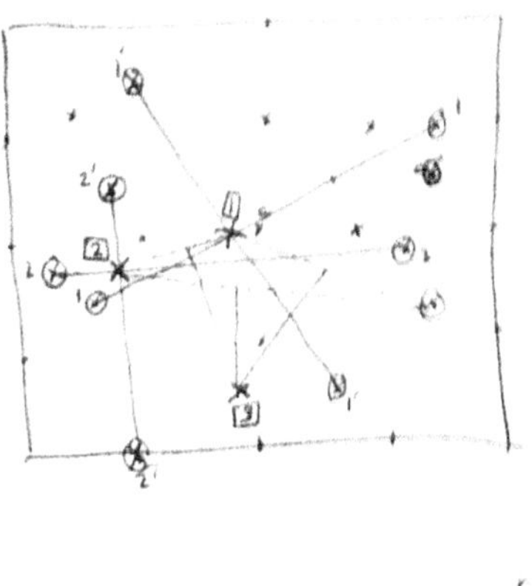

I visited **Sol Lewitt** in his Hester Street studio and he copied the instructions for *The Location of Three Points* wall-drawing while I was there. It was a piece that he had not quite finished and he was thinking it through toward the end. In fact he had to cross out the word "upper" and replace it with "lower". He also quickly sketched it out as a small drawing to make sure the instructions would, in fact, locate three points that actually would fall within the confines of a wall. I had seen a Lewitt wall-drawing show being installed by students at Gallery A-402 at CalArts in the spring of 1972. One of the students, Matt Mullican, was drawing an "endless line" for which he was using a mechanical pencil so he could go on and on and on, all over the wall. My own execution was in a fairly hard pencil, on a wall about six feet wide, about eight feet into the apartment and facing the door as you entered. It was a difficult feat but quite satisfying. Afterwards, I enjoyed coming and seeing this wall that so specifically contained an extra layer of ideation, even though it was barely visible. I didn't even photograph it because it wouldn't have shown up. Later I saw a show of Sol's wall-drawings being installed in the 420 building, probably at John Weber. They were being elegantly executed by a Japanese artist (or team), who thereafter did many of his drawings, I heard. As poorly attended as the Project Inc. shows usually were in Cambridge, the attendance dropped further for the Weston shows, as Weston was a good half hour ride from town. The only person who came to Sol's show was Alex Grey, perhaps the most famous American artist who no one in the art world has heard of. He loved it. One reason I like Sol Lewitt's work so much is that anyone anywhere in the world who wants to can install a Sol Lewitt in their home or any wall. Anyone can "have" (if not "own") an important artwork for free.

Above, a sketch of Sol Lewitt's wall-drawing *The Location of Three Points*

THE LOCATION OF THREE POINTS
WALL-DRAWING

THE FIRST POINT IS LOCATED WHERE TWO LINES WOULD CROSS IF THE FIRST LINE WERE DRAWN FROM A POINT WHICH IS HALFWAY BETWEEN A POINT WHICH IS HALFWAY BETWEEN THE CENTER OF THE WALL AND THE MIDPOINT OF THE LEFT SIDE AND A POINT WHICH IS HALFWAY BETWEEN THE MIDPOINT OF THE LEFT SIDE AND THE LOWER LEFT CORNER TO A POINT WHICH IS HALFWAY BETWEEN THE CENTER OF THE WALL AND THE UPPER RIGHT CORNER AND A POINT HALFWAY BETWEEN THE MIDPOINT OF THE RIGHT SIDE AND THE UPPER RIGHT CORNER, THE SECOND LINE IF IT WERE DRAWN FROM A POINT HALFWAY BETWEEN A POINT WHICH IS HALFWAY BETWEEN THE CENTER OF THE WALL AND THE MIDPOINT OF THE BOTTOM SIDE AND A POINT WHICH IS HALFWAY BETWEEN THE MIDPOINT OF THE BOTTOM SIDE AND THE LOWER RIGHT CORNER TO A POINT HALFWAY BETWEEN THE POINT HALFWAY BETWEEN THE CENTER OF THE WALL AND THE MIDPOINT OF THE TOP SIDE AND THE UPPER LEFT CORNER.

THE SECOND POINT IS LOCATED WHERE TWO SETS OF LINES WOULD CROSS IF THE FIRST LINE IS DRAWN FROM A POINT HALFWAY BETWEEN THE POINT HALFWAY BETWEEN THE END OF THE FIRST LINE AND ITS' INTERSECTION POINT AND A POINT WHICH IS HALFWAY BETWEEN THE MIDPOINT OF THE RIGHT

SIDE AND THE LOWER RIGHT CORNER TO A POINT HALFWAY BETWEEN THE MIDPOINT OF THE LEFT SIDE AND THE BEGINING OF THE FIRST LINE OF THE FIRST SET, THE SECOND LINE IS LOCATED HALFWAY BETWEEN A POINT HALFWAY BETWEEN THE END OF THE SECOND LINE OF THE FIRST SET AND A POINT HALFWAY BETWEEN THE MIDPOINT OF THE LEFT SIDE AND THE UPPER LEFT CORNER AND A POINT HALFWAY BETWEEN THE CENTER OF THE WALL AND THE MIDPOINT OF THE LEFT SIDE TO A POINT HALFWAY BETWEEN THE CENTER OF THE WALL AND A POINT HALFWAY BETWEEN THE MIDPOINT OF THE BOTTOM SIDE AND THE LOWER LEFT CORNER

THE THIRD POINT IS LOCATED EQUIDISTANT TO THE FIRST AND SECOND POINTS AND A POINT WHICH IS LOCATED HALFWAY BETWEEN A POINT HALFWAY BETWEEN THE CENTER OF THE WALL AND THE MID-POINT OF THE RIGHT SIDE AND A POINT HALFWAY BETWEEN THE MIDPOINT OF THE RIGHT SIDE AND THE ~~UPPER~~ LOWER RIGHT CORNER. SOL LEWITT/2/23/74

PROJECT INC.
MAY 24, 1974
8 PM

SHOW AT: TRAPELO HOUSE
CAMBRIDGE SCHOOL
WESTON, MA. 02193
617-891 5885

Tom Marioni
February 18, 1973

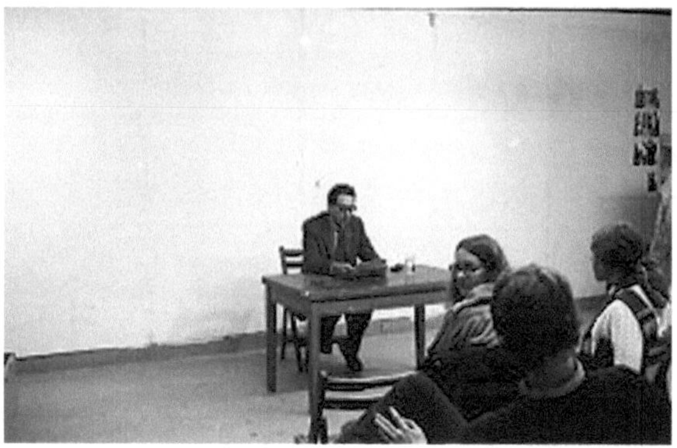

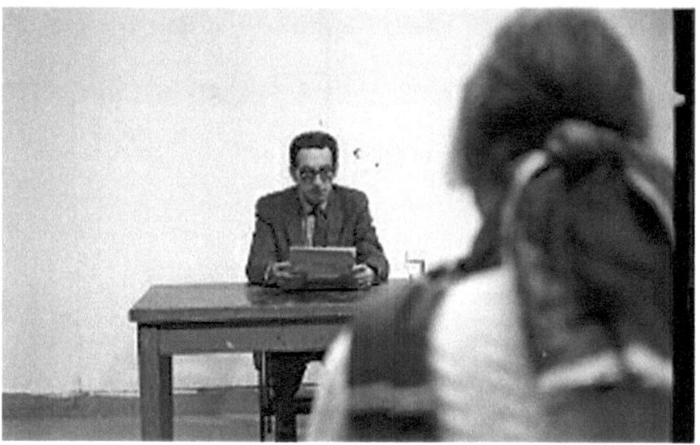

In 1973, **Tom Marioni,** conceptual artist and proprietor of the Museum of Conceptual Art in San Francisco, did a performance in absentia at Project Inc. He hired an actor, who showed up the night of the performance; a well dressed, gray haired man with glasses. The actor read from an autobiographical text by Marioni while seated behind a table. In the text, which was about fifteen minutes long, Tom, through the actor, told a few stories about himself and his family, including, I think, the claim that his grandfather invented ice cream. The performance took place under white lights and no refreshments were served, nor was there any music. In succeeding years, as Tom honed his statement he began performing in yellow light, perhaps because of its resonance with beer.

On May 11, 2012, his performance in absentia took place under yellow light and beer was served as the actor, a young woman, read excerpts from Tom's memoir, *Beer Art and Philosophy* (2003) while piano jazz (Solo Monk) played in the Villa Metamorphosis, Ben Ryuki Miyagi's fantasy vacation house in Saugerties, NY. This was the kickoff event of Project Inc. Revisited.

Above, an unidentified actor performing as Tom Marioni at Project Inc., 1973

Paul McMahon

December 8, 1972

PAUL McMAHON
performances objects

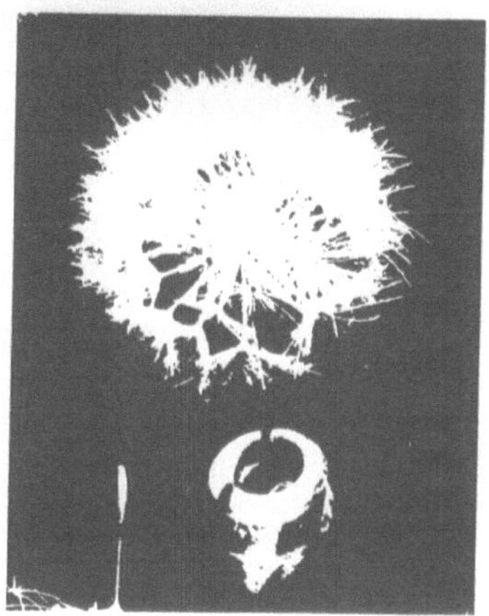

One night a thief stele my safety razer frem its shelf in the bathreem cabinet in my derm. Lying in its place he left this pieture.

Dec.8, 8pm at
Project Inc.
141 Huron Ave.
Cambridge
(near Concord Ave. on the trolley)

This is the **second** in a series of contemporary art shows, events and performances organized by Paul McMahon in co-operation with PROJECT INC. 141 Huron Ave. Shows will take place there every Friday night at 8pm throughout the foreseeable future. Important New York artists will show as well as Boston artists. $1 donation asked not demanded. There will be no show on Dec. 1.

SCHEDULE INFO: Paul McMahon...492-4438
PROJECT INC....491-0187

I showed about ten works from the previous year or so, and did three short performance pieces. One of the things I showed was a change of clothes that I put on brand new and wore until they wore out.

Robert C. Morgan
November 24, 1972
& July 26, 1975, with Barbara Hero

ROBERT MORGAN
three other events

bongo burner boiling out bongo burner boiling in
burner bongo boiling out burner bongo boiling in
out boiling burner bongo in boiling burner bongo
boiling out burner bongo boiling in burner bongo
bongo boiling burner out bongo boiling burner in
out burner boiling bongo in burner boiling bongo
burner boiling out bongo burner boiling in bongo
boiling burner out bongo boiling burner in bongo
boiling burner bongo out boiling burner bongo in
burner boiling bongo out burner boiling bongo in
burner out boiling bongo burner in boiling bongo
boiling bongo burner out boiling bongo burner in
boiling out bongo burner boiling in bongo burner
out boiling bongo burner in boiling bongo burner
burner bongo out boiling burner bongo in boiling
bongo burner out boiling bongo burner in boiling
boiling bongo out burner boiling bongo in burner
burner out bongo boiling burner in bongo boiling
out bongo burner boiling in bongo burner boiling
bongo out burner boiling bongo in burner boiling
bongo out boiling burner bongo in boiling burner
out bongo boiling burner in bongo boiling burner
out burner bongo boiling in burner bongo boiling
bongo boiling out burner bongo boiling in burner

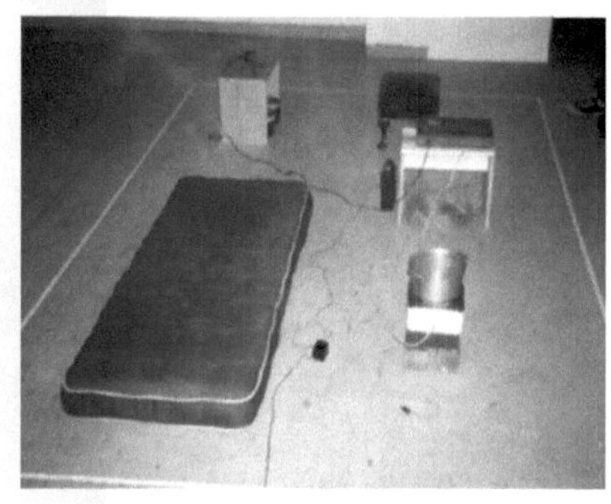

Robert C. Morgan opened and closed the series, peculiarly enough. Bob was the closest to a like mind that I could find in Boston, which I really couldn't. But we respected each other's ideas very much. Bob came from abstract painting and I came from conceptual art and blues guitar.

His work derives more from his interest in painting than from other performance art. He still considers himself a painter, though his recent work has been in the form of performance events. Three Other Events utilized the bongo drums, electric burner, and boiling water on the flyer as well as a tape recorder, rope, stopwatch, and other things. He created relationships between the things and himself, acting slowly and deliberately in a ritualistic way.

No one remembers the last show in July 1975; neither Morgan nor Barbara Hero, who shared the show with Bob, nor I. It was a total surprise when Helene Winer hired me to be her Assistant Director in the fall of 1975, so there was no sense of this as "the last show."

As a student at Pomona I referred to myself as a synaesthesiologist, and aesthetic crossbreeding was the intention of Pomona's Experimental Residency Project and later the Disney's inspiration for CalArts, though it never gained traction in either case. Barbara Hero, now 86, is a true synaesthesiologist with a long track record, which I only discovered in preparing for this show.

Above: the setup for Robert Morgan's *Three Other Events*, 1972

Matt Mullican
December 1, 1973
& February 16, 1975

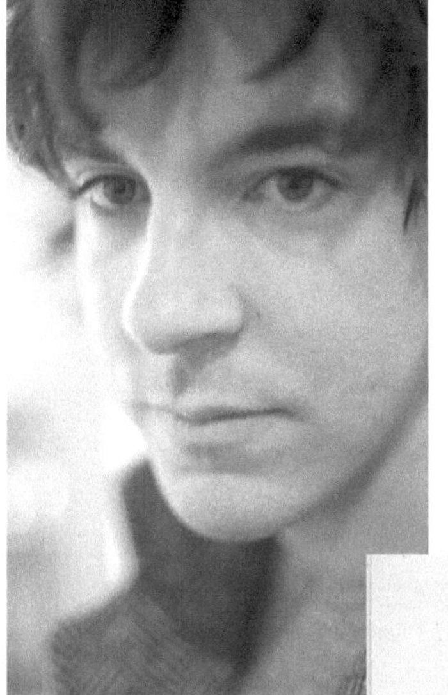

Matt Mullican at BCAE c. 1975

Below, Matt Mullican, *Fates Arm*, 1973

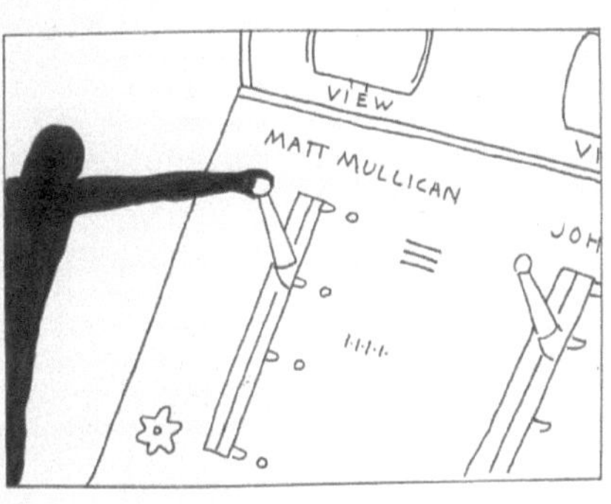

Around 1972, **Matt Mullican** was in Westbeth, illegally subletting from XX (name withheld to protect the guilty, who was illegally subletting from someone else, etc.) He had a huge insight and saw what he then considered his next five years' work. It was more like twenty. By the time he got to Project he had been working on it for about a year. His show contained dozens of drawings, including stick figures and dead people. He did performances involving degrees of self-hypnosis. On the wall next to him was a large line drawing of a corner, and he visualized what was around the corner. He saw a girl named Cindy. He and Cindy Sherman were later a couple for a while. He also did a performance where he visualized himself walking into the landscape of an old engraving of a Roman scene with an arch and woods. He entered and talked about how it looked and felt. After a while I, who was holding the picture up for Matt to see it, lit it on fire. Matt, inside the picture, reported on what it was like with the fire coming and as it got more and more uncomfortable before he eventually died, if memory serves.

He later came back and did a performance at MassArt. He used the students who came as part of the work but didn't tell them what they were representing. They were cast as a Soul, escorted by Death, and contested by an Angel and a Demon, appearing before God, on top of the table, and the Devil below it, or something very close to that. I thought it was interesting that he never told the students what they represented. Only I was told.

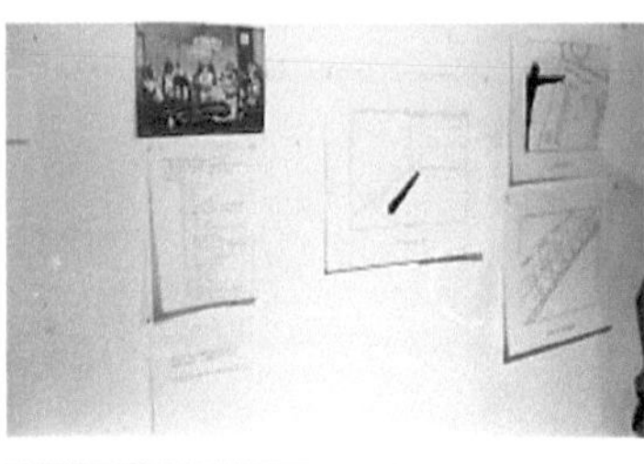

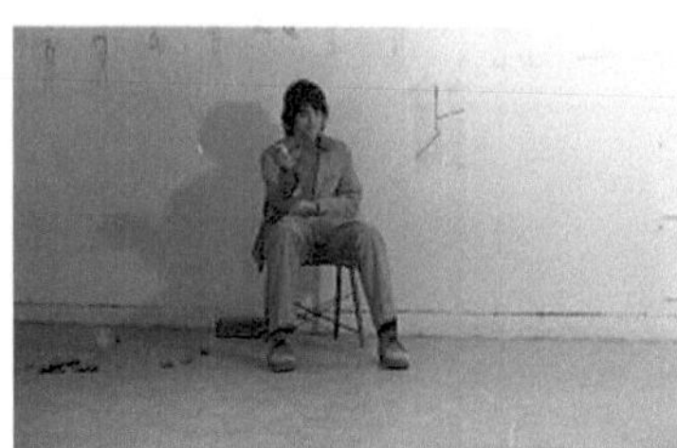

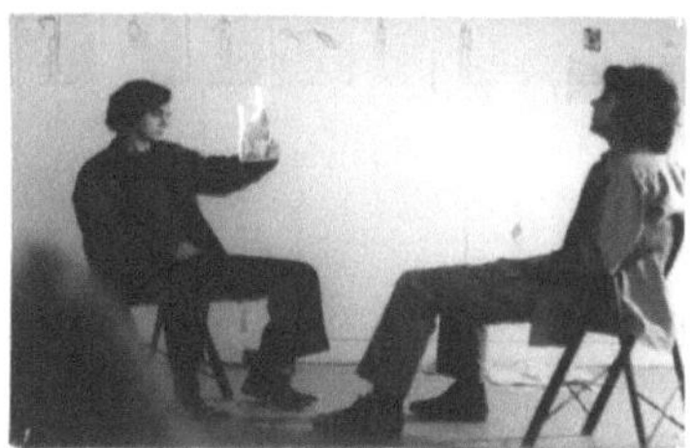

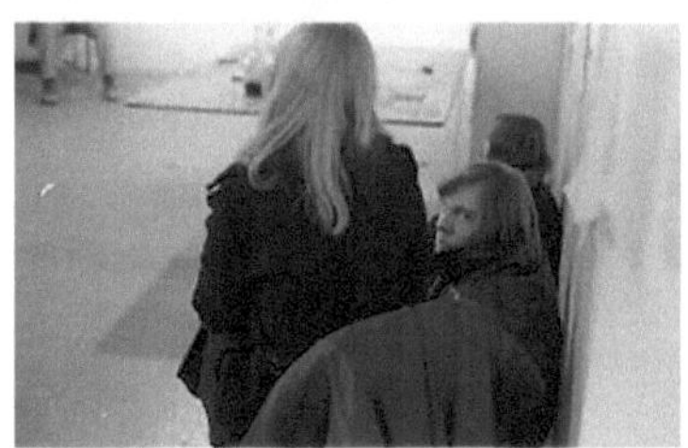

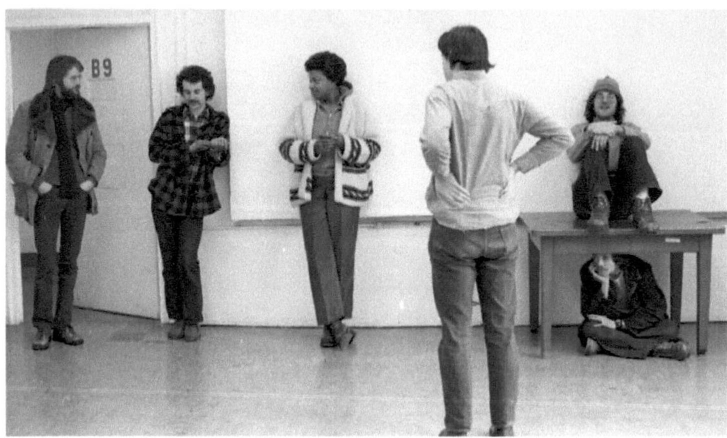

top left: installation; works on paper, 1973
top right: Matt Mullican performing
middle: Matt Mullican assisted by Paul McMahon; visualizing himself inside an old engraving, which is set on fire
bottom: Matt Mullican and students at MassArt

Dean Nimmer
October 20, 1973

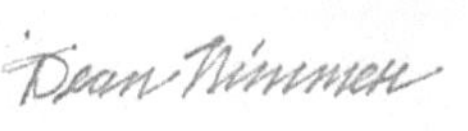

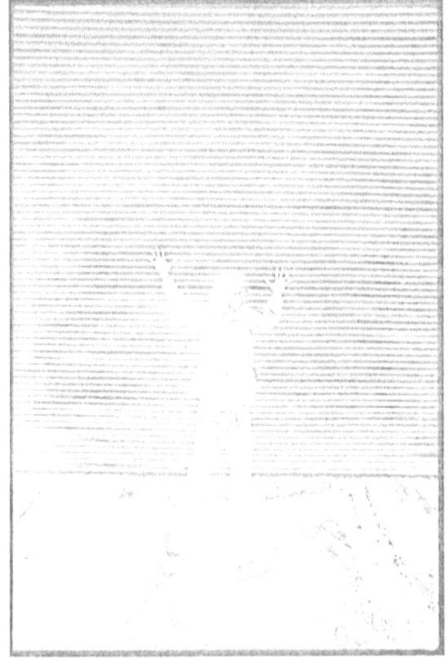

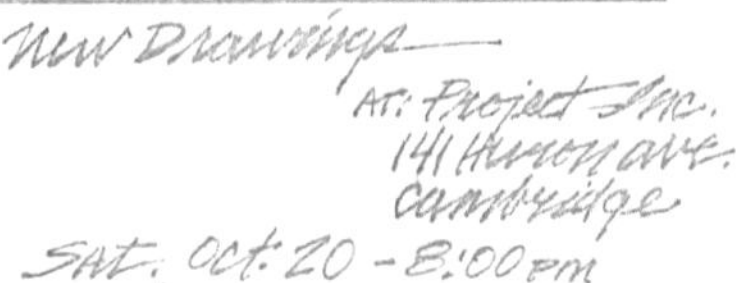

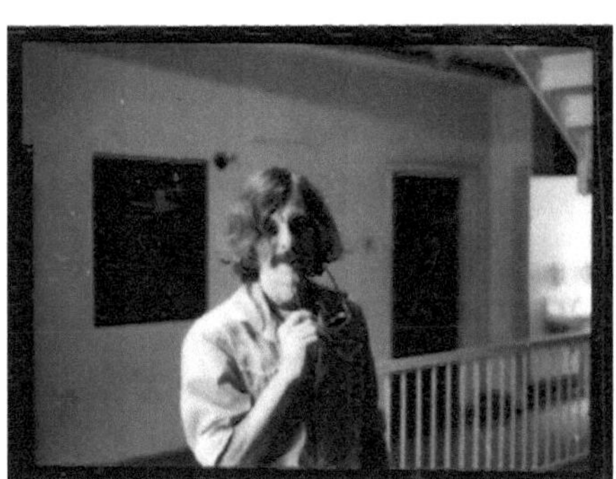

Dean Nimmer taught both my mother and me how to paint using watercolors. He taught me twenty or thirty years before he taught my mother. I actually made two very good-looking watercolors in his class. Then I wasn't interested in doing more and haven't done much since that summer in 1973. My mother, on the other hand, is knockin' 'em out. With Greg Amenoff, Dean produced funny art-themed sketch comedy and ironically, had a game show called *Beat Your Mother At Art*. It was rigged so the mothers always won but in our case my mom won fair and square.

David Salle
March 15, 1975

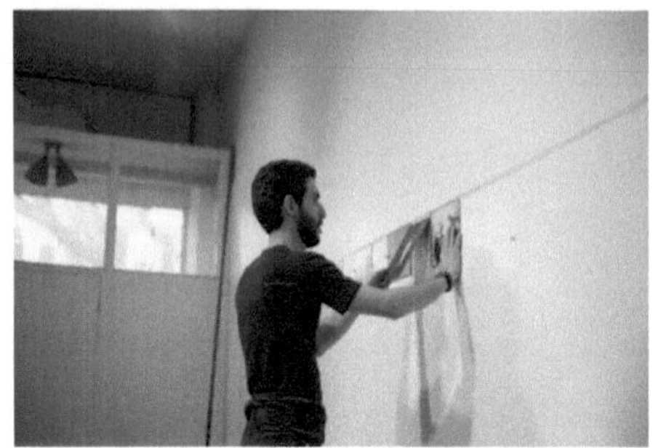

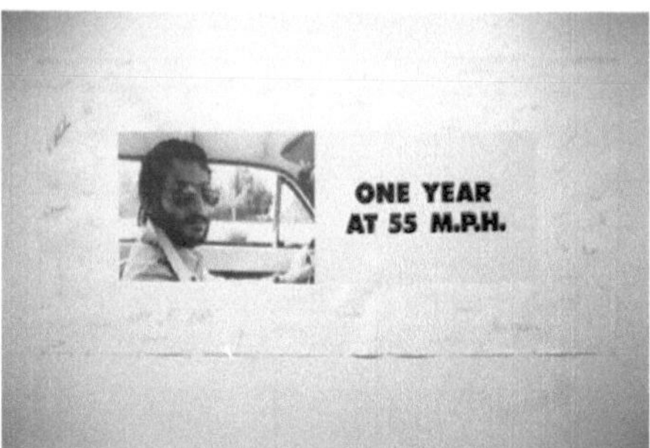

David Salle is one of the sharper tools in the toolshed. I had heard a lot about him from Matt Mullican and Jim Welling. They had a great respect for him, especially since as an underclassman he was accepted into Max Kozloff's class. We exchanged letters but I didn't meet him until March 1975, when he knocked on my door and I opened it. He was wearing impossible glasses, huge and Italian, with the estimable Susan Davis in tow. He was clearly the most ambitious person I ever met, relentlessly driven and focused. His work was pointedly perceptive and assertive, asking a lot of questions about a lot of things. Alone among the artists who showed, he got critic Kenneth Baker, who had written about *Indian Summer* (the September 1974 group show featuring Salle's *Coffee Drinkers*) in the *Boston Phoenix*, to attend, and they talked intently for a very long time. Alas, no review.

In his solo show Salle showed *One Year At 55 MPH*, which had been signed by viewers at an earlier show and which we all signed as well. There were also some "prettier" pieces involving (rephotographed?) black-and-white photos of water at night, collaged with pictures of artists' models and flowers. David cultivated a vaguely sinister undertone and there was one remarkably disturbing work: a matrix of four photos of the same woman's butt with a different color circle painted around the anus in each. It was not painted on the photograph, it was painted on the person and then photographed. Toward the end of the show two men came in who gave me the creeps. They had the sort of feeling like they could have been undercover cops or something. High testosterone levels. They didn't look like artists and they planted themselves in front of the anus piece and kept looking at it for a very long time. I was freaking out because I had no idea why they were staring at it so long. They probably just liked porn. Anyway, I very firmly closed the show exactly at ten, shooing everyone out, and they left.

Willoughby Sharp
March 1, 1975

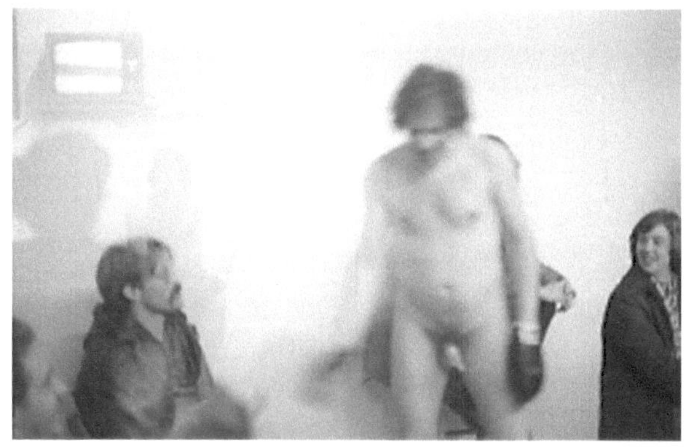

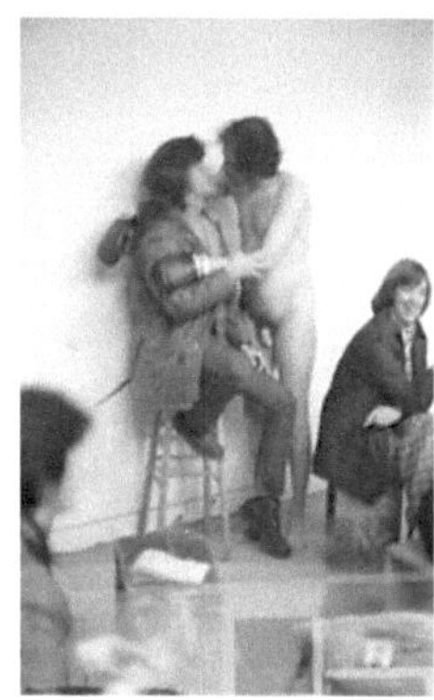

Willoughby Sharp truly was the mighty mogul he claimed to be among all of us who self-identified as the hippest portion of the art world. He was a crucial publicist and connector of people and scenes.

Avalanche was "the" performance/conceptual art magazine and I was very happy to have been mentioned in the gossip column "Rumbles" in the same spread with Jay Jaroslov's arrest story. Willoughby essentially wrote me a letter telling me he wanted to show at Project Inc. and didn't let me weasel out of it like I wanted to. I was single-mindedly attempting not to show anything I wasn't 100% behind and I hadn't seen evidence of genius in Willoughby's work yet. When we did the show I was shocked at how many people showed up. The place was filled to the rafters with local artists who never came to the shows. Then I realized they thought he could make them famous. Willoughby, bless his soul, had other things in mind. The back wall did not go all the way up to the ceiling. The director's small loft office overlooked the main space with a large open window about ten feet up. Willoughby set a large video monitor on a high shelf where everyone in the main space could see it. The subject matter was dysfunctional family relations exposed, I think. Willoughby dropped acid and got naked. Then he walked through the crowd. It was quite an amusing sight. Perhaps because he was tripping it was hard to really get a grip on what was going on. He made his way over to the ladder to the loft office and started climbing it while getting hysterical, repeating some role-playing line like, "Mommy, why don't you answer me?" His intensity increased as he climbed into the office, where the monologue shifted to searching: "I'm going to find you. I know where you are. I'm going to come and get you!" He started acting like he thought there was someone inside the wall that he needed to reach. When he started pounding a hole with a brick in Trintje Janssen's funky old lath and plaster wall I stopped him. I knew how hard it was to patch when the lath was broken and I also knew who was going to be patching it.

Willoughby's performance may not have knocked me out, but he himself was quite lovable and beyond picturesque. A glorious Vincent Price type, dressed like Jack the Ripper with a big black hat and high black leather boots, as brash as it gets, well organized and always on the make. Long may he be revered for his service to the creative principle. He was very upset with me for stopping his performance and said it had never happened to him before. I had never done it before either, and I never have since.

Above and right: Willoughby Sharp performing at Project Inc., 1975

Charles Simonds
February 1975

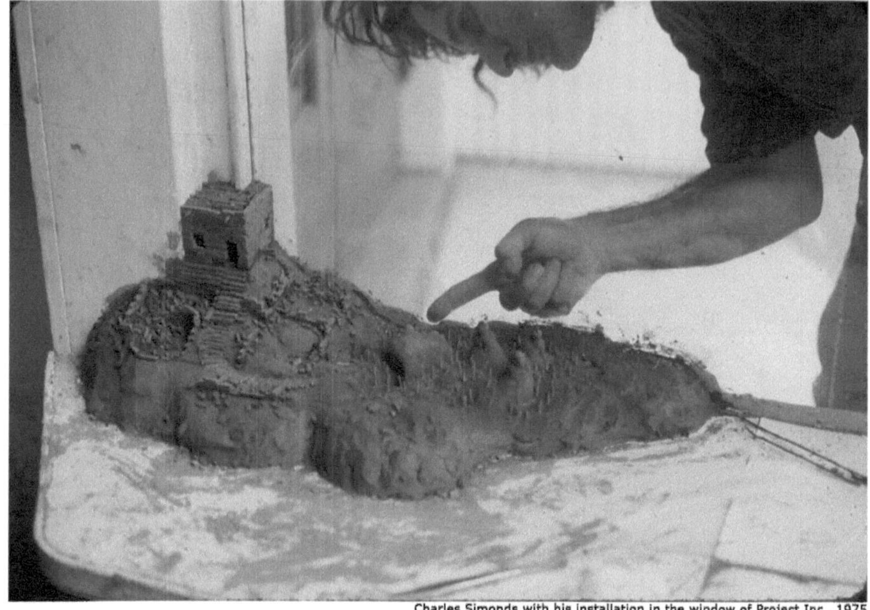

Charles Simonds with his installation in the window of Project Inc., 1975

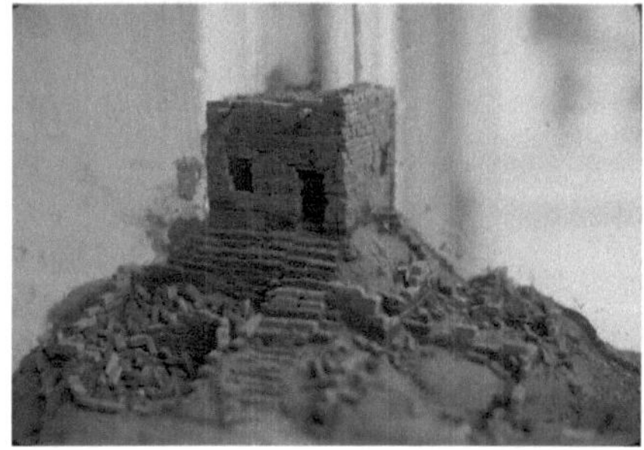

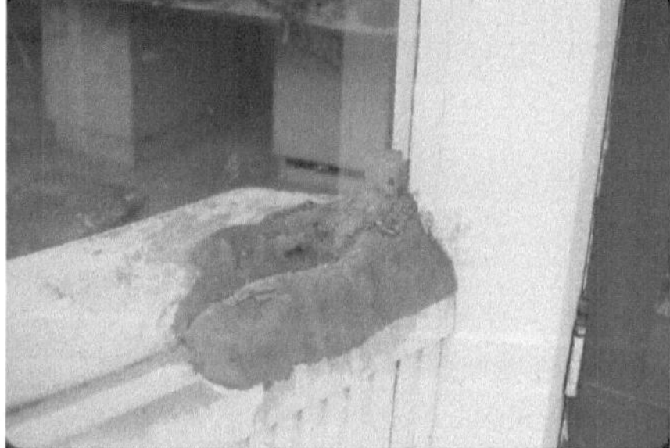

Charles Simonds was an early and delightful street artist, whose miniature settlements and ruins made of tiny red clay bricks were mysteriously appearing in cracks in the walls on the Lower East Side and today may be found in the stairwell of the Whitney Museum. He was willing to spend a day, or possibly two, in the window of Project Inc. installing a fantastic little village, most of which was inside the plate glass window. There was a narrower section on the outside of the glass, in the street, just to the left of the front door. It stayed up for a month, the longest show at Project Inc.

Alan Sondheim
December 7, 1974
& April 1, 1975

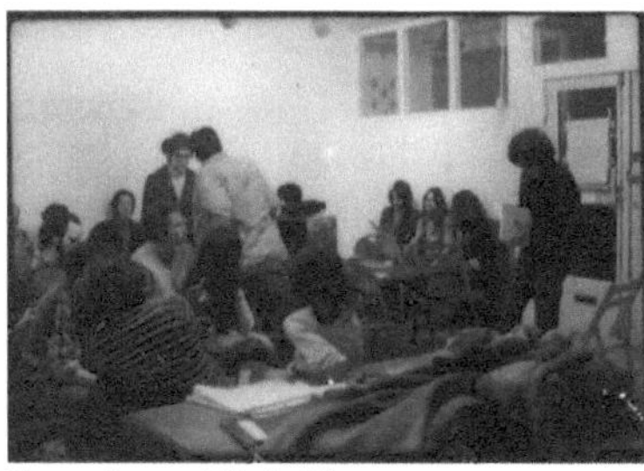

The audience at Project Inc.

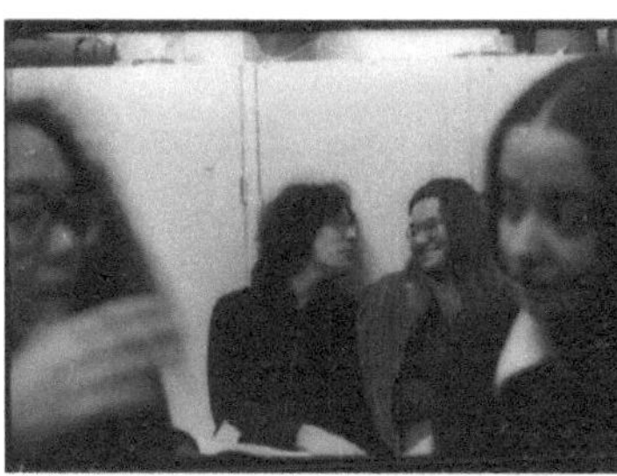

Loretta Staples, Alan Sondehim, Rosemary Mayer, and Adrian Piper

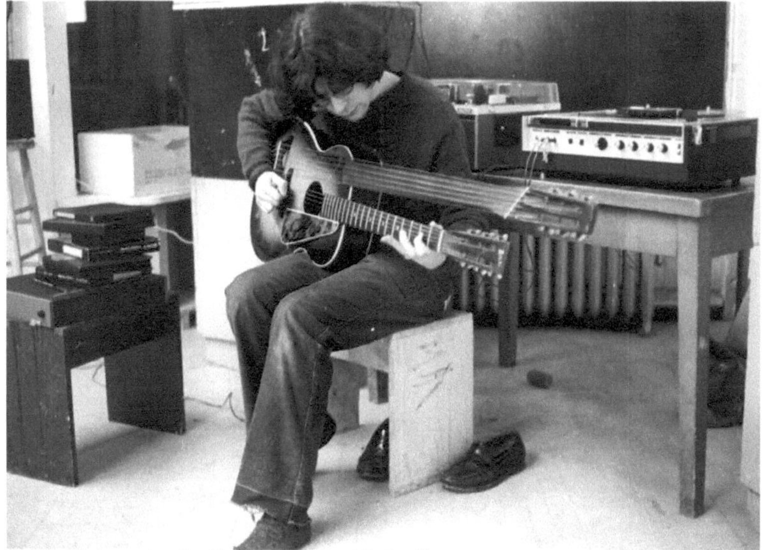

Alan Sondheim performing *The World's Fastest Guitar Player*

I think it was at **Alan Sondheim**'s first show that he brought some students from RISD, where he taught, including Mary Boone, who remembers meeting me but I don't remember meeting her. Also in that crowd were Adrian Piper and Rosemary Mayer, as well as Robert Horvitz, who held a little reception for Alan after one of the shows. The centerpiece was a pate in the shape of the United States with the words "Downwardly Mobile" written on it.

Wolfgang Stoerchle
March 29, 1973

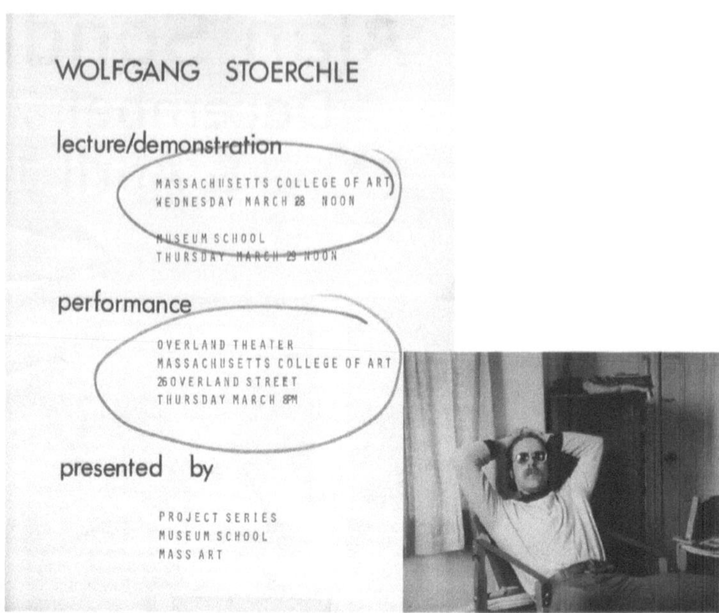

WOLFGANG STOERCHLE

lecture/demonstration

MASSACHUSETTS COLLEGE OF ART
WEDNESDAY MARCH 28 NOON

MUSEUM SCHOOL
THURSDAY MARCH 29 NOON

performance

OVERLAND THEATER
MASSACHUSETTS COLLEGE OF ART
26 OVERLAND STREET
THURSDAY MARCH 8PM

presented by

PROJECT SERIES
MUSEUM SCHOOL
MASS ART

Wolfgang Stoerchle and his brother rode horseback across the United States. He came to California to study with Matt Mullican's father Lee Mullican at UCLA but went to Santa Barbara where he and Robert C. Morgan were art student friends. His work often centered on his penis and was controversial, causing repercussions in the world. I scheduled a performance for him at MassArt. In this performance there were different sections. Toward the end Wolf stood naked and blindfolded, facing the crowd in a darkened room with light only on him. After he stood there for a while, his uncircumcised penis began to stir. Without any other part of him moving, his penis started to slowly become erect. It bobbed up a little bit and the down, then up a little higher. He got about halfway up. I was amazed that anyone could do that. Others were amazed too, and also outraged. The understanding was that this would be the first in a series of performances at MassArt. This was attractive to the artists because of the possibility of a larger audience and because MassArt was willing to pay a small honorarium. Wolf's show both began and ended that series. Transgression for its own sake was not Wolf's attitude, but the penis is the third rail where civilized behavior is trumped by instinctual reactivity and people simply freak out.

I had reviewed his performance a year earlier at Pomona. Maybe that's why he invited me to his place in Santa Barbara. We drove up there in his Mercedes from CalArts one day in the spring of 1972. He lived in an old mission style Spanish building that housed a Catholic school for girls. He lived in a corner apartment, a veritable garret overlooking the courtyard where Catholic girls in uniforms came and went between classes. It strained credulity that this was his habitat. It was too perfect. He had a portable video machine and showed me a bunch of reel-to-reel ¾-inch black-and-white tapes. At first I wasn't sure what part of the body I was looking at. There were little hairs and a lump of flesh slowly moving, slowly unwinding; it was a penis wrapped in a scrotum, slowly getting closer to emerging, which it finally does, but what emerged first from its uncircumcised head was a tiny Disney character figurine, which the penis finally ejected. This process was repeated for a series of different characters: Mickey, Donald, Goofy. The obvious subtext is that CalArts was Disney's brainchild.

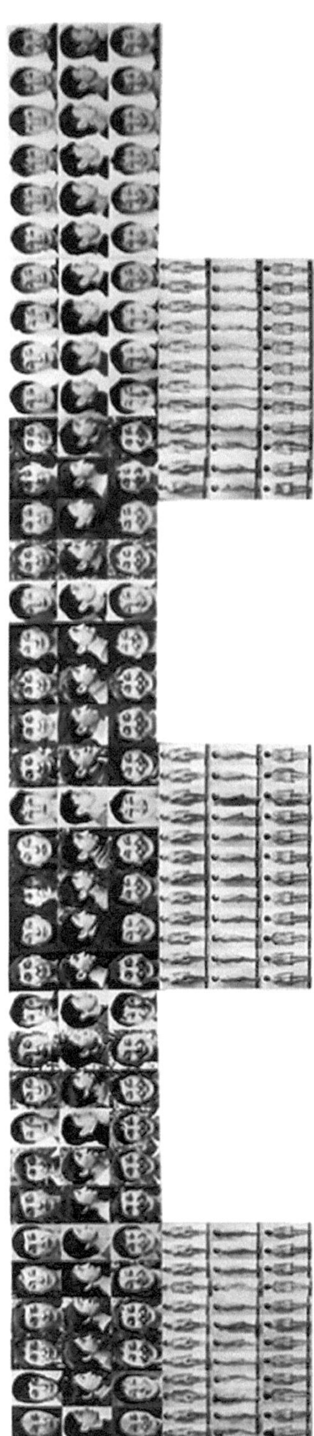

Athena Tacha
May 4, 1974

Exploration of Self, A show of photographic and textual studies by ATHENA TACHA, including

Who is Athena?, 1973
Split Selves, 1973
Nuances of Feelings, 1972
Phases of Laughter, 1972
Four Weeks of Changing Behavior, 1972
Three Months of Dreaming: A Journal of My Nights, 1972

May 4, 1974 8 pm
Project Inc.
141 Huron Ave.
Cambridge, Ma.
891-5885

Athena Tacha showed a piece that aggregates pictures of her taken regularly to document the changes in her face and body over time. As the piece continues it will be shown in its current state at the Churner and Churner show. See: Postcards by Artists.

Lawrence Weiner
May 12, 1973

Lawrence Weiner - Publications

Date	Title	Publisher & Availability
1968	STATEMENTS	Published by Siegelaub/Kellner NYC
1970	TRACES	Galleria Sperone, Corso san Maurizo 27, Torino
1971	ART & PROJECT/LAWRENCE WEINER	Art & Project, van Breestr. 18, Amsterdam
1971	10 WORKS	~~XXXXXXXXXXXXXXXXXXXXXXXXXXX~~ Yvon Lambert, 15 rue L'Echaudé Paris 6
1971	FLOWED	Nova Scotia College of Art & Design 6152 Coburg Road, Halifax Nova Scotia, Canada
1971	CAUSALITY: AFFECTED AND/OR EFFECTED	Leo Castelli, 420 West Broadway NYC
1972	HAVING BEEN DONE AT/ Having been done to	Galleria Sperone, Corso san Maurizo 27, Torino
1972	A PRIMER	Published by Documenta 5 available from: Buchhandlung Walther König, Breitestr. 93, 5 Köln
1972	GREEN AS WELL AS BLUE AS WELL AS RED	Jack Wendler, 164 North Gower Str. London NW1
1972	7	Recorded and released by Yvon Lambert 15 rue L'Echaude Paris 6
1973	WITHIN FORWARD MOTION	Kabinett für Aktuelle Kunst, Karlsburg 4, Bremerhaven, Germany
1973	ONCE UPON A TIME	Galleria Toselli, Milano Via Melzo 34, Milano Italy

Lawrence Weiner showed all of the books he had published up until then. I visited him in New York to discuss the show, which he was not able to attend in person. He talked about making enough books over his lifetime to fill a shelf about six feet long. That way when he died, the books would be like a same-size surrogate for him.

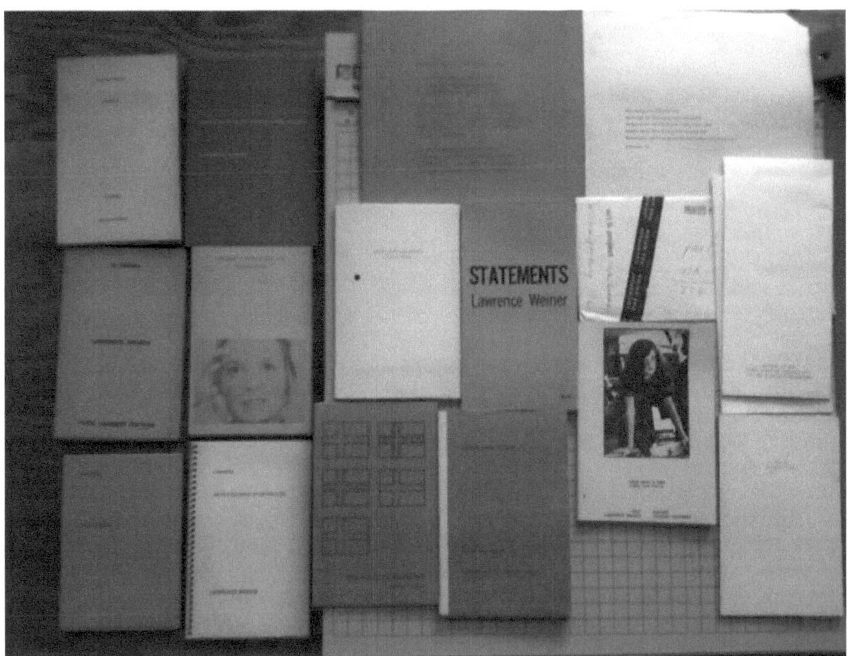

Publications by Lawrence Weiner

James Welling
January 19, 1973
& December 17, 1974

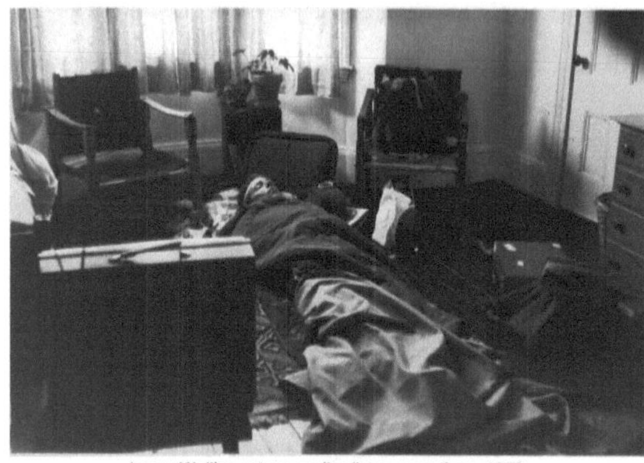

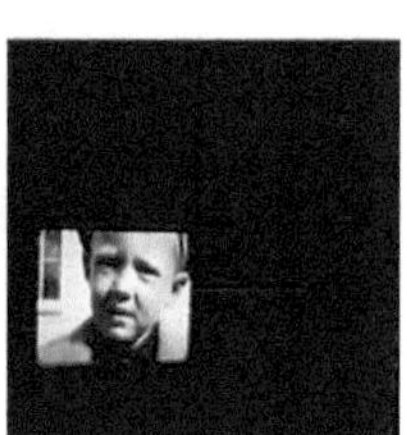

James Welling asleep on the living room floor, 1973

James Welling was a teaching assistant at the California Institute of the Arts and a crucial participant in the shows at Project Inc. His sensibility was the closest to mine and he was in and out of our apartment and neighborhood constantly from the beginning through the summer of 1975. He showed his work in a series of small, dark, and cluttered rooms in the basement of Project Inc. In the first room, which was empty and fairly well lit, he mounted a retrospective of his work. In the next three rooms he did a piece dealing with his ancestors. He put each generation in a different room. By walking through the rooms, one moved back in time. He used objects owned by his ancestors, pictures of them, written material about and by them, furniture made by them, etc. Upstairs in the storefront space, videotapes by students from CalArts ran continuously and the audience moved freely from one show to the other.

Besides his first show, Welling also showed the following year at MassArt. He showed an elaborate mélange of slide projections and video monitors with mysterious and evocative imagery whose subjects was a marina he could see out his window in Venice, California. He called it *Boatyard*.

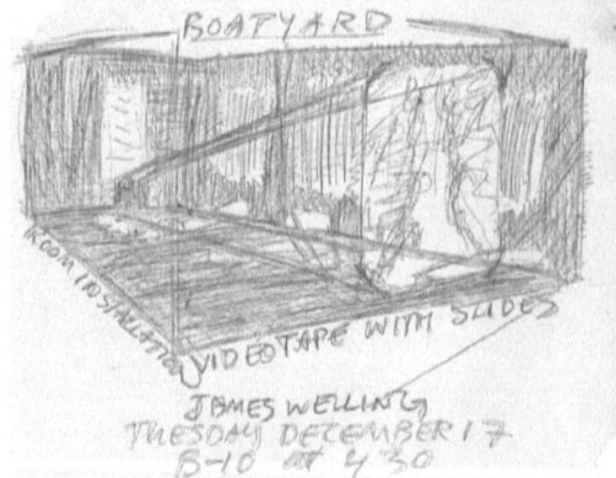

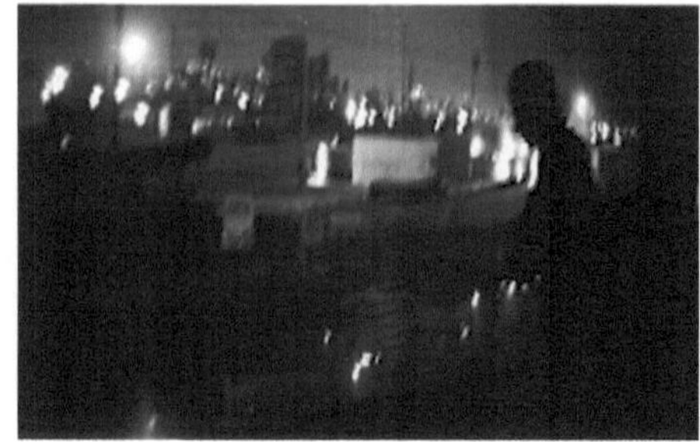

Boatyard installation, with James Welling in silhouette

Martha Wilson
April 7, 1973

MARTHA S. WILSON

APRIL 7 AT 8 PM

PROJECT INC.
141 HURON AVE.
CAMBRIDGE, MA.
02138

SELFPORTRAIT

Credibility equals reality, so that "self" depends not on who you think you are, but on who others think you appear to be. In the space below, write your impressions of me, and return the slip to the box at the door. In so doing, you are creating me, and subverting the meaning of the term "selfportrait".

Martha S. Wilson

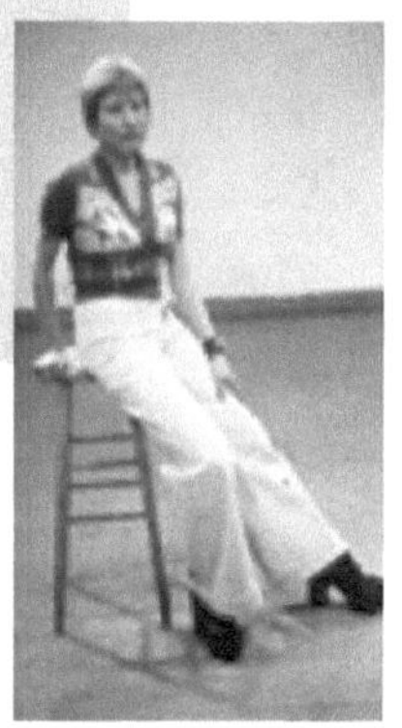

Martha Wilson did the piece that appeared on the flyer for the show, entitled "Selfportrait." The instructions were: "Credibility equals reality, so that 'self' depends not on who you think you are, but on who others think you appear to be. In the space below, write your impressions of me, and return the slip to the box at the door. In doing so, you are creating me and subverting the meaning of the term 'selfportrait.'"

Above, Martha Wilson in performance

CHURNER and CHURNER

IMAGE CREDITS

pp. 10 - 13, 14, 18, 20, 24, 25, 29 top, 33 bottom, 34, 37 bottom, 38, 45, 48 left, 49 left, 52, 55, courtesy of the Project Inc. Archive at the Bard Center for Curatorial Studies, Bard College,
Annandale-on-Hudson, New York

All other images courtesy of the artists and Paul McMahon

All original Project Inc. documents courtesy of Paul McMahon

ACKNOWLEDGEMENTS

Paul McMahon would like to thank the Churner sisters, Rachel and Leah, and, for his tireless work on this project, Ian Wallace.

Thanks to Ann Butler and the CCS for providing a good home for the Project Inc. archive.

Thanks to David Platzker and Jean-Noël Herlin for their guidance and Douglas Eklund for rediscovering this territory.

Thanks to Helene Winer, Barbara Reise, John Baldessari, and all of the artists who showed at Project Inc., especially Dan Graham.

And thanks to Jody Winer for all her help.